# ¡Alabadle!

# ¡Alabadle!

## Hispanic Christian Worship

Edited by
Justo L. González

Abingdon Press
Nashville

¡ALABADLE!

*This book is printed on recycled, acid-free paper.*

**Library of Congress Cataloging-in-Publication Data**

Alabadle! : Hispanic Christian worship / edited by Justo L. González.
    p.    cm.
    ISBN 0-687-01032-2 (alk. paper)
    1. Hispanic Americans—Religion.   2. Public worship.
I. González, Justo L.
BR563.H57A42    1996
264'.0089'68073—dc20                                                    96-4134
                                                                          CIP

Scripture quotations, unless otherwise indicated, are from the New Revised Standard Version Bible, copyright © 1989, by the Division of Christian Education of the National Council of the Churches of Christ in the United States of America.

The lines from "Tenemos Esperanza (We Have Hope)" in chapter 7 are reprinted with permission from Discipleship Resources, Nashville, TN.

Permission has been granted by Abingdon Press for use of *Nuestro Credo (Un Credo Hispano)* and the *Hispanic Creed,* on pp. 114-15.

Permission has been granted by Friendship Press for use of *A Thanksgiving Litany* on p. 116, and for "*Las Posadas*" on p. 117.

Permission has been granted for use of words and music for "*Padre Nuestro*" on p. 118, by the Mexican American Cultural Center in San Antonio, TX.

96 97 98 99 00 01 02 03 04 05—10 9 8 7 6 5 4 3 2 1

MANUFACTURED IN THE UNITED STATES OF AMERICA

# CONTENTS

Introduction . . . . . . . . . . . . . . . . . . . . . . . . . . . . . . . . . 7

1 Hispanic Worship: An Introduction . . . . . . . . . . . . . . . 9

Justo L. González

2 Hispanic Catholic Prayer and Worship . . . . . . . . 29
Allan Figueroa Deck, S.J.

3 Hispanic Pentecostal Worship . . . . . . . . . . . . . . . 43
Samuel Solíván

4 Worship in the
Hispanic United Methodist Church . . . . . . . . . 57
María Luisa Santillán Baert

5 What Is Different About
Hispanic Baptist Worship? . . . . . . . . . . . . . . . . . . 73
Miguel Angel Darino

6 Becoming a Mestizo Church . . . . . . . . . . . . . . . 89
Teresa Chávez Sauceda

*7* An Introduction to Hispanic Hymnody . . . . . . *101*

Raquel Gutiérrez-Achón

Appendix: Worship Resources. . . . . . . . . . . . . . . *111*

Pablo A. Jiménez

Notes. . . . . . . . . . . . . . . . . . . . . . . . . . . . . . . . . . . *125*
Glossary . . . . . . . . . . . . . . . . . . . . . . . . . . . . . . . *131*

# INTRODUCTION

As a project, this book began to evolve at the 1994 Biennial Assembly of the Asociación para la Educación Teológica Hispana. (The Asociación, also known as AETH, is a voluntary association of some four hundred Latinas and Latinos committed to the task of theological education among our people, at all academic levels and for a variety of ministries.) At that gathering, a number of us read and discussed papers that eventually led to the essays now compiled in this book. We critiqued and encouraged one another. We prayed and played together. And in so doing we developed a book that has more inner unity than most edited volumes.

The list of authors shows the variety and unity of which I speak, which we have experienced. *Dr. Allan Figueroa Deck, S.J.,* of the Center for Pastoral Studies at Loyola Marymount University, is also Executive Director of the National Association of Catholic Hispanic Ministries. *Dr. Samuel Soliván,* an ordained minister in the Assemblies of God, is Associate Professor of Christian Theology at Andover Newton Theological School. The *Rev. María Luisa Santillán Baert,* an ordained United Methodist minister and a member of the Rio Grande

Conference, has served in various capacities, both in local churches and in national staff positions, as well as in Mexico and in the Channel Islands. She currently pastors in Dallas. *Dr. Miguel Angel Darino,* an American Baptist minister, is Regional Minister of Hispanic Ministries for the American Baptist Churches of the Pacific Southwest. The *Rev. Teresa Chávez Sauceda,* an ordained Presbyterian minister, is currently completing her doctoral degree at the Graduate Theological Union in Berkeley, California. *Professor Raquel Gutiérrez-Achón* serves as Editor for the Spanish Hymnal Ecumenical Committee. *Dr. Pablo A. Jiménez,* who has compiled the worship resources at the end of the book, is an ordained minister of the Christian Church (Disciples of Christ) and currently serves as Executive Director of the Asociación para la Educación Teológica Hispana. I am an ordained United Methodist minister, and a retired member of the Rio Grande Conference of The United Methodist Church.

Each of us represents a different perspective and a particular experience of worship. Yet together we believe that the Hispanic church has a significant contribution to make to the entire church. It is in that spirit and with that hope that we now launch this book. The pages that follow represent the wide variety of Hispanic Christian worship. Yet, in the midst of that variety we find unity. It is that unity in variety, as well as our excitement in worship, that we wish to communicate to our readers and to the church at large. We are excited about this book, because we are excited about worship; and we are excited about worship, because we are excited about the gospel!

# CHAPTER ONE

Justo L. González

# Hispanic Worship

## An Introduction

### The Many Faces of Hispanic Worship

Who is a Hispanic? How do they worship? These questions are not easy to answer. There is no such thing as a typical Hispanic, or a typical form of Hispanic worship. Yet perhaps it is in that very multiplicity—in the impossibility of defining and describing us as a whole—that our greatest contribution to the church at large lies.

Besides the distinctions that divide every ethnic group—gender, class, level of education, and so forth—there are three others that are of crucial importance for the Latino community. (Here, as throughout this volume, the terms "Hispanic" and "Latino or Latina" are used interchangeably.)

The first of these distinctions has to do with countries of origin and cultural background. The largest group among

Hispanics are those whose cultural roots are in Mexico. Some of these people had ancestors in the southwestern United States before this area became U.S. territory as a result of the Mexican-American war. Others have come across the border at various times since. Generally, they are most numerous in the West and Southwest, although in the last two decades their numbers have been increasing in the Midwest and throughout the nation. The second largest group is the Puerto Ricans, concentrated in the Northeast, but also quite numerous in the Midwest, and found as far away as Alaska and Hawaii. Other groups come from Cuba, the Dominican Republic, South America, and particularly in more recent times, Central America. Although these various Latino subgroups speak a common language, there are differences in vocabulary, foods, music, and a host of other cultural aspects. Also, as these groups meet one another and interact, there are younger generations whose parents belong to different subgroups, and who are therefore Hispanics whose roots are found in more than one country of origin. Thus, one could say that a new form of being Hispanic—a form that includes traits from all Latino subgroups—is slowly emerging in the United States.[1]

These cultural differences are reflected in worship. For instance, Latino churches of the same denomination may use maracas and bongo drums, or mariachi music, depending on whether they are in New York or in Texas. In Los Angeles, a church potluck supper may include Salvadoran *papusas,* while in Boston there might be Puerto Rican *mofongo* or Cuban *congrís.*

Second, the Latino religious community is often divided along generational lines. Older people and more recent immigrants tend to prefer Spanish, while many in the younger generations prefer English. Teenagers in particular are often ashamed of being "different" from their peers, or from the dominant culture that they see on TV, and therefore avoid speaking Spanish. The resulting dynamics in congregations is quite interesting, and sometimes sad.

Often the congregation is the only place where the older generation of Latinos and Latinas have a voice—they are generally disempowered in politics, and very seldom can they influence the schools where their children attend or the curricula they follow. Therefore, many older Hispanics are tempted to turn the church into a cultural preserve, whose main function is to transmit the mother culture to the younger generations. When that happens, the younger folk—especially teenagers—resent being forced to worship in Spanish and to follow the traditional culture, with the result that as they grow up they often leave the church—at least for a while. Thus, the generational conflicts that are so common in the dominant culture—and which are not as marked in Hispanic cultures themselves—become quite divisive in many Latino congregations.[2]

Other congregations move in the opposite direction. Since their children seem to prefer English, and since the younger adults who are most fluent in English are also economically the most successful in the community, these churches conduct all programs for children and youth in English, and eventually move as far away as possible from their Latino roots. In consequence, they are no longer able to welcome the new immigrants and their children, who must then find other communities of faith and other places to worship.

Third, the Latino community is divided by denominational loyalties in a way that is quite different from what happens in the dominant culture. Latino Protestantism, both in Latin America and in the United States, has grown mostly on the basis of anti-Catholic preaching and teaching. Among many Hispanics, to be a Protestant means to be anti-Catholic, so often Roman Catholicism is depicted in the worst light possible—they are idolaters who worship the Virgin and the saints, they do not believe in the Bible, they believe that they can save

themselves through their own good works, their interpretation
of the Eucharist is cannibalistic, priests are tyrannical and
immoral, and so on.

At the other end of the spectrum, there are Hispanic Catholics who seem to believe that the Roman Catholic Church has
a monopoly over Hispanics, and that a Latino or Latina who
becomes a Protestant is a traitor to our common heritage. Some
of these people are quite accepting of Anglo Protestants—after
all, that is what Anglos are supposed to be—but they see any
Protestant growth in the Latino community as unwarranted
proselytizing and an infringement of the basic rules of ecumenical etiquette. (One could say in passing that it is precisely
this attitude that has been a major contributor to the growth
of Protestantism and the defection among Hispanics from the
Catholic Church. Those among Roman Catholics who hold
this attitude tend to take Hispanics for granted as members of
the Catholic Church—and no one likes to be taken for
granted.)

Thus, Hispanic worship has many faces according to the
various combinations of these three factors. The possible combinations are numerous, and each impacts worship in a particular way. Think, for instance, of a Mexican Roman Catholic
parish composed mostly of persons who prefer to worship in
Spanish and who still have deep roots in Mexican culture. In
that parish, the Mass will be central, probably in Spanish with
mariachi music, and perhaps even some liturgical dances pat-
terned after ancient Mexican religious dances. Also, some
elements of the traditional Mexican popular religiosity will be
present—the Virgin of Guadalupe, *posadas,* the *Via Crucis,* and
so forth.[3]

In the same neighborhood there may be a Pentecostal
church whose doctrine is staunchly anti-Catholic, but whose
members come from the same strata of society as the majority
of those in the Catholic church. Instead of the Mass, their
worship will center on preaching, praise, *testimonios, coritos,*

and prayer for healing.[4] The *coritos,* however, will most likely be sung to the accompaniment of a mariachi-style band, rather than Caribbean-style maracas and drums. Also, it is quite likely that some of the people who attend this church, and whose rhetoric is rabidly anti-Catholic, will have an image of the Virgin of Guadalupe at home. In the same community, there may be a "mainline" Protestant church whose worship is mostly in English and follows the general pattern of Anglo churches of the same denomination. Still, when they celebrate a baptism they do so with a number of elements unknown in Anglo congregations, but quite common in the Mexican tradition—godparents, special dresses and foods, and practices of *compadrazgo.*[5] In that same church, there may be a time set aside during the worship service for *coritos,* and they may also sing some songs taken from the mariachi Mass normally sung down the street. Meanwhile, at the other end of the country, in New York, similar combinations are taking place, although in a different context since the Mexican influence is not as powerful as the Puerto Rican or the Dominican.

In brief, there are many faces to Hispanic worship, and any attempt to describe that worship without taking that variety into consideration would be false.

On the other hand, as one travels throughout the nation and worships, as I have, in a wide variety of Latino contexts, one senses a commonality that somehow holds these various strands together. Latino churches, whether Catholic or Protestant, whether mostly Mexican, Cuban, or Salvadoran, have their own particular flavor in worship. It is this flavor that I shall seek to explore in the rest of this chapter, and which is then illustrated in its various incarnations in the chapters that follow.

However, before moving on to that subject, there is an important caveat to be made. There are a number of churches—relatively few, and mostly very small—whose membership is mostly Latinos and Latinas, but whose worship is

scarcely distinguishable from what takes place at eleven o'clock
in predominantly Anglo congregations of the same denomination. There is a place for such churches, since obviously people
who worship there find that these churches meet their needs
and relate to their own stance within the cultural gamut in the
United States. Yet they are not included in this essay—nor in
the rest of this book—for obvious reasons: If they are like any
other church, and their worship is no different, there is little
need to study their worship or what it might contribute to the
church at large.

**Worshiping as Pilgrims and Exiles**

If there is an experience that unites Hispanics in the United
States, it is the experience of belonging, yet not belonging.
There are many ways to describe that experience. Among
Latinos and Latinas, the most common are probably *mestizaje*
and exile.

The term *mestizaje* cannot be easily translated into English.
In colonial times in what is now Latin America, a *mestizo* (or
*mestiza,* if it was a woman) was a person of mixed Spanish and
Native parentage. A *mulato* (or *mulata*) was a person of mixed
Spanish and African parentage. *Mestizaje,* therefore, is the
quality of being *mestizo* (or *mestiza*)—and *mulatez* is the
quality of being *mulato* (or *mulata*). It was Fr. Virgilio Elizondo, of San Antonio, who applied the category of *mestizaje*
to the Mexican-American experience, and employed it as a tool
for sociological, psychological, and theological analysis.[6] At a
later time, as Black pride and the notion of *negritude* have
gained currency in theology, similar reflections have taken
place, mostly among people of Caribbean origin, around the
subject of *mulatez.*[7]

Elizondo points out that being a *mestizo* puts one beyond
the margins of dominant definitions. From the point of view
of the Spanish, the *mestizo* is an Indian. From the point of view

of the Indian, the *mestizo* is Spanish. In many ways, the *mestizo*'s very existence is a challenge to the neat divisions and classifications that are used to justify the existing status quo of exploitation and segregation. As a result, the *mestizo* is exploited by the powerful Spanish, and segregated and rejected by both the Spanish and the Indian. The *mestizo* is nobody. And yet, the *mestizo* is the sign of the future, for the new nations being born out of the colonial crucible—in the particular case of Elizondo's example, Mexico—will be neither Spanish nor Indian, but *mestizo* nations. And, what was true then of the original *mestizos* of Mexico, where the Indian and the Spanish element met, is now true, says Elizondo, of the Mexican-American, who is a new form of *mestizo*—now neither Mexican nor American, and both Mexican and American. Therefore, in short, *mestizos* do not belong; and yet, they belong to the future, for what they now are is what the rest of society is to be.

Although originally stated as an analysis of the Mexican-American condition and consciousness, the notion of *mestizaje*—and its parallel *mulatez*—has struck a responsive chord among Latinos and Latinas of various backgrounds, as a way of understanding and stating their condition in this country and society. Furthermore, if *mestizos* pose a challenge to the accepted definitions of what people are or ought to be in any culturally segregated society, Hispanic *mestizaje* poses a particular challenge to the United States, which is long accustomed to thinking only in terms of Black and White. We are not White, even though some of us may be blond and blue-eyed. Nor are we Black, even though some of us may have all the traits of purely African descent. We are a race that is not a race in any of the traditional senses. Thus, our very existence points to the mythical and ideological character of the very notion of "race": Contrary to what we are told, racism is not the outcome of race, but vice versa. In other words, it is not race that gives rise to racism, but racism that gives rise to the very notion of "race."

Another way of expressing the experience described as *mestizaje* is the image of exile. Obviously, many Hispanics are in this country as exiles. Even those who did not come here as political refugees are in many ways exiles—just as even those who cannot claim mixed blood are nevertheless *mestizas* and *mestizos*. An exile is a person living in a foreign land, and unable to return to the land of origin. Many Hispanics are literally in that condition, due to tyranny and civil wars in their own countries. But even those who originally came to this land seeking economic improvement are also exiles, for they cannot in reality go back—even were they to return to their native lands, much of what they knew would no longer be there, and in any case they themselves are no longer the same people they were when they first left.

The image of exile is complex, and so are the sentiments it evokes. Clearly, in most cases one's sentiments toward the land of exile are not altogether negative. To the degree that one had any choice in the matter, the land of exile is also the land that appeared—and probably was—most welcoming, most able to receive one who for whatever reason had to leave the native land. At the same time, however, the word *exile* implies not really belonging. The exile's real home is elsewhere—or was elsewhere, for commonly the exile has no home to return to. If a *mestizo* lives, so to speak, "at the hyphen" (the hyphen between "Mexican" and "American," or between "Cuban" and "American"), the exile lives between parentheses, waiting for the probably-never-to-come time of return.

For Latinas and Latinos who were born in this country, the image of exile expresses the manner in which the dominant society often looks at them. They are made to feel as if they are not at home, invited in many subtle ways to "go home," when in fact they have never known any other home than this. Those who have come from other lands often find themselves living in the midst of a community that cannot understand that, in spite of their decision to leave those lands, they still love them and long for them. All of us find that, even when our neighbors of the dominant culture make their best efforts to receive and include us, we still do not quite belong.

All of these experiences affect worship, and how we relate to it. For one thing, there is probably no place where the feeling of exile and alienness becomes more poignant for me than when I attend worship in most Anglo churches of my own or another "mainline" denomination. Here I am among sisters and brothers in Christ. I believe what they believe, and seek to stake my life on the same faith on which they stake theirs. Most of them are friendly and loving people who have every intention of making me feel included and at home. I am in church, the spiritual home for the homeless of which 1 Peter speaks.[8] And yet, I am not at home. Quite often, even in the midst of such worship, I find myself athirst, "as a deer longing for flowing streams," and repeating the words of the psalmist:

> These things I remember,
> as I pour out my soul:
> how I went with the throng,
> and led them in procession to the house of God,
> with glad shouts and songs of thanksgiving,
> a multitude keeping festival. (Ps. 42:4)

This is a painful experience—painful, not only because of the feeling of not belonging, but also because I know how hurt the people with whom I am worshiping would be if I told them of my feelings. Thus I sit quietly and politely, and in the best of cases what should have been an act of corporate worship becomes a time of private devotion and reflection.

Obviously, some of this sense of not belonging has to do with cultural and aesthetic gaps. I am profoundly aware of the role that culture plays in worship—a matter to which I shall return later. I know, for instance, that although I am bilingual, and know English grammar better than most native speakers, I still am not stirred by poetry in English as I am by poetry in my own native tongue. But my sense of not belonging is much deeper than that.

As I sit in a worship service, reflecting on why it is that I do not quite belong, the great contrast that strikes me is that this church and its people are, so to speak, "installed," while my people and I see ourselves as pilgrims, both out of theological conviction and out of sheer necessity. When in a Latino church we say "Thy Kingdom come," we say it with deep and almost desperate longing. When it is said in some of the churches of the dominant culture, one almost hears a whispering undertone: "but not just yet." The reasons are obvious: If one is quite content in the existing order, there is no need to look forward to God's Reign. But if, on the other hand, one is in exile or a *mestizo,* living so to speak "at the hyphen" of *mestizaje* or between the parentheses of alienness, one longs for change, for a new future, for "a new heaven and a new earth." At best, one can pitch a temporary tent in the present, as the children of Israel did in the desert.

During the last century, in reaction to the mistakenly otherworldly emphasis of much traditional Christian piety, theologians and preachers have been emphasizing the positive value of the world. That is an important emphasis that must not be lost. As Christians, we are not to be like that philosopher of old who fell into a well because he was gazing at the stars. We must be engaged in the life of this world, seeking to make the political and the economic order as just as possible. That is all true and quite important. *But* this does not mean that we are to be placidly installed in this world and its present order, as if the Reign of God had already come—or even as if the present order were a reasonable facsimile thereof. The notion of the people of God as a pilgrim people is crucial to the Bible, "for here we have no lasting city, but we are looking for the city that is to come" (Heb. 13:14). As Christians, we are a people of the future—a people of the future Reign from which and toward which God calls us. If we lose that, we are as salt that has lost its flavor.

Christian worship is, among other things, the place where we catch a glimpse of that future—a glimpse that both supports us in our pilgrimage and judges us in our attempts to be too settled. In the Eucharist, as we share food, we commit ourselves to a life of sharing, "until he comes" (1 Cor. 11:26). In baptism, we are grafted into the resurrected body of Jesus, and thus share in his resurrected life. In preaching, we announce to ourselves and to the world God's promised Reign of love, peace, and justice. In singing, we practice for the day when we shall "laud and magnify" God's glorious name "with angels and archangels, and with all the company of heaven," as we now say at communion.

For worship to be all of these things, however, we must have a clear sense that we are a pilgrim people; that we can never be fully installed in this world or in this society and its present order; that for us, as a second-century Christian would say, "every foreign land is as a homeland, and every homeland is foreign."[9]

Thus, part of what we as Hispanics bring to worship—and part of our contribution to the worship life of the church at large—is the painful experience of not quite belonging, which is the counterpart of the joyful experience of belonging to God and God's Reign! Our very existence, and the witness of our churches in our barrios, is an invitation to the entire church to become a pilgrim people, and to learn to worship "on the march."

**Worship as Fiesta**

Reading the chapters that follow, one senses that the common thread running through all of them is the celebrative character of worship. I remember being told some years ago about a professor of worship in one of our seminaries becoming upset over a comment from a Latina in one of his courses. She had majored in theater, and had worked for some time as a director in a small neighborhood theater. One day, she blurted out: "This course is very similar to some that I took in drama school, but not quite as good. I thought that worship was supposed to be a celebration, not a performance."

Perhaps this student was not quite fair in her description of the course she was taking. But, as I reflect on some of the customs and practices that I see in Anglo churches in "mainline" denominations, I see that there is much truth in what she was saying. I find, for instance, worship leaders more concerned about where various participants are to stand, or how the choir is to process, than with the actual content of the good news we are supposed to be celebrating. I find congregations where people just sit and stare—or stand and fidget—as the gospel is being read, and then when the organ finishes playing the postlude, they break forth in applause (presumably because they find the postlude more exciting than the gospel?). I am surprised to see people barely nod when they hear that Christ is risen from the dead, and then jump and shout when their team scores a touchdown. I find people complaining if the service is not over in exactly sixty minutes, and then get excited when a basketball game goes into overtime. I even find myself sitting in such worship services, sometimes in the middle of communion, looking forward to the benediction and the dinner that comes later. And we are supposed to be celebrating the Event of the Ages?

Latino worship is a fiesta. It is a celebration of the mighty deeds of God. It is a get-together of the family of God. It is important to remember this in order to understand some of the features of our worship that sometimes disconcert or even upset those of the dominant culture.

First of all, because worship is a fiesta rather than a performance, it may be planned, but not rehearsed. Oftentimes,

Hispanic worship seems chaotic. Indeed, there are some Hispanic pastors and other leaders who are remiss in that they do not even plan the celebration, but simply let it happen. But in most cases the difference between our worship and that of the dominant culture is that we think in terms of planning a party more than rehearsing a performance. Certainly, choirs and bands rehearse; but the service, as such, is never rehearsed. We plan, as one does for a fiesta, in order to make sure that the necessary arrangements have been made. In the case of a fiesta, one arranges for enough food and chairs, for a mariachi or some other kind of music, and for parking. But one cannot actually plan all the details, as one does in a performance, because the success of the fiesta depends on the attitude and participation of those present, not just on the performers. Likewise, in worship, the celebration is the people's fiesta, and therefore the pastor and other worship leaders can plan only up to a point, leaving the rest to the celebrants themselves—and, as many Hispanics would stress, to the guidance of the Holy Spirit.

The very word *celebrant* is significant. In traditional ecclesiastical jargon, the "celebrant" is the one who presides. That is tantamount to calling the singers in a fiesta, or the master of ceremonies, the "celebrants." The fact is that in worship all participants are "celebrants," in that they are gathered to celebrate the fiesta of God and God's people. In this respect, Roman Catholic Latino worship has changed drastically since the days before Vatican II. When I was growing up, devout Catholics used to say that they were going to "hear" Mass—*voy a oír misa*. To them, the Mass was a performance—a supernatural performance, but a performance nonetheless—in which the priest and his entourage participated while the rest of the people watched and listened. But after Vatican II all of this changed. Most Hispanic Roman Catholic Masses in this country now reflect the culture of the people, and engage the people in active participation. In order to promote that participation, several Latino Masses have been produced, many of them with direct involvement of the worshipers in the creative process.

Sometimes people in the dominant culture complain that our worship is too emotional, too festive. We reply that all the books about worship state that we must offer God our best music and our best art, and we feel that there is nothing in the world as worthy of celebration as the gospel—the Good News of Jesus Christ. Therefore, we must give God in worship the fullest of our emotions and the liveliest of our celebration.

Furthermore, in our culture the most significant fiestas are connected with a sense of family—of an extended family that includes all sorts of relatives, and whose limits are never clearly defined. This is not a closely knit, tightly defined, and exclusive family, as when we speak of the nuclear family in the dominant culture—a family where one main value is privacy. It is rather a vast assemblage of people who are related in a multiplicity of ways, so that they have a sense of belonging, but not necessarily of excluding others. In this sense, our worship is a family celebration. We gather as God's children, to celebrate the new birth that makes us such, and in a large measure to celebrate having one another as family. At this point, it is important to remember that for many of us, as exiles and wanderers in this land, the extended family that is so important in our culture is no longer a reality. Therefore, the church often takes on this role. We gather to worship and to celebrate, very much as in the old country relatives from all over a valley would gather to celebrate Pancho's baptism, Josefa's wedding, or just being a family. That is one reason why in many of our churches there is a service practically every night. Our people need that sense of family in order to survive in an alien world; they need to celebrate God's future in the midst of an oppressive and alienating present. To those from well-installed positions in the present social order who would call this escapism, we reply that theirs is the true escapism—living and acting as if they could at once claim the gospel and ignore its promised future of love and justice.

A fiesta is characterized by movement and by sensuality. Significantly, this point is made in the chapters that follow, although with different words, by Allan Figueroa Deck when speaking of Catholic piety, and by Samuel Solivan when speaking of Pentecostal worship. Often the room or sanctuary is decorated with vivid colors, and filled with the sounds of music and the smells of food. The people move around. They dance. They embrace. They shout. They cry. They laugh. They eat and they drink. Much of this is reflected in our worship.

In the chapter on Pentecostal worship, Dr. Solivan speaks of windows decorated with plastic to make them more colorful. In many churches the walls are decorated with quotations from scripture, with children's art, or with banners. All of these somehow remind us that we are part of this large family that is celebrating its great reunion. When we enter, there is sound—not always soft music—reminding us that this is the fiesta of the people of God. In many of our churches, both Catholic and Protestant, we move to rhythm as we sing—or at least we clap our hands to rhythm. In some cases, people seem to be almost dancing to the tunes of the hymns, the *coritos,* or some typical rhythm that has been adapted for worship. At times they are actually dancing. In Catholic churches as well as in some others, the smell of incense is part of the celebration.

Our church members tend to be very interactive. We embrace as we arrive; we embrace during the passing of the peace; and we embrace again before we leave. When the time comes for sharing concerns before intercessory prayer, many of us speak about things that in other circles would be considered too private to be discussed in such a large company. In prayer, many lift their hands to heaven. Others cross themselves. Still others sway as if moved by an imperceptible breeze. Some mumble their prayers, producing a hum throughout the con-

gregation. Others cry out in longing or in joy. Sometimes more
than one person prays out loud. In many cases, it is impossible
to tell all that is going on. But then, the same is true of any
good fiesta!

### Multicultural Worship

When I visit churches of the majority culture and speak of
Hispanic worship, or of the rapid growth of Latino churches,
the question often arises of multicultural worship. There is a
legitimate concern behind that question, for the goal of Christian worship is that day when "a great multitude that no one
can count, from every nation, from all tribes and peoples and
languages," will worship together, "standing before the throne
and before the Lamb" (Rev. 7:9). Thus, the fact that today we
find it difficult to worship together across cultural lines should
cause us significant disquiet.

There are many issues at stake here—issues of faith and
culture, of culture and language, of worship and aesthetics, and
of aesthetics and culture—and this is not the place to try to
resolve them. But at least there are some hints that Hispanic
worship may offer to the church at large.

The first of these is that we must reevaluate critically much
of what we have inherited from the Reformation and, even
more, from the Enlightenment. The Reformation quite rightly
insisted on the value of worship in the vernacular. But then the
Enlightenment led us to a view of worship in which there is
no place for that which cannot be clearly understood. The
reason for the use of the vernacular, we were told, is that people
must understand what is being said and what they are saying
in worship. Otherwise, worship becomes gibberish and
mumbo jumbo.

There is much truth in that view. Certainly, worship that
does not engage the mind fails to engage the entire human
being. We must hear the Word of God with at least sufficient

understanding that we may know what it is that God requires of us; and we must also hear it with sufficient understanding that we may have at least a glimpse of what it is we are gathered to celebrate.

But there is also a grave error in that view, which reduces human nature to the intellectual. There is much we do not understand that is nevertheless of great significance to us. (It is said that Pablo Picasso, upon hearing a man comment that he could not understand one of his paintings, asked, "Sir, what did you have for lunch today?" "Why, steak," said the man. "Did you enjoy it?" asked Picasso. "Certainly," came the reply. To which Picasso then asked, "And, did you understand it?") I do not need to understand Dvorak's Fifth Symphony in order to enjoy it, and I don't have to enjoy Wagner's music in order to be overcome by it. Yet much Protestant mainline worship seems to be based on the premise that what is significant in worship is what we understand—to which perhaps is added a bit of music we can enjoy. That is why children are so often left out. In a Presbyterian church that I attend occasionally, children are given "worship activities" to entertain them while the adults go about the business of worship. That is also why the uneducated and the illiterate are excluded along with the children. There is no mystery left to cut us all down to size, to make us like those little children to whom belongs the kingdom of heaven. We think that we are excluding the children, the uneducated, and the unsophisticated, when in truth we are excluding ourselves—or, we exclude them from our worship, and thereby exclude ourselves from the heavenly banquet.

This is where the Latino worship experience may be able to make a significant contribution to the church at large. Fiesta and mystery go together. In a fiesta, as in a steak dinner, we are not required to understand everything that goes on. We are not even expected to agree with everything that everyone says. We are simply invited to join the party, to allow ourselves to be carried and defined by it, to make our own contribution, whatever that might be, and above all to celebrate whatever the fiesta is about. In churches representing different Latino sub-groups—which are rapidly increasing in numbers—several variants of Spanish are spoken. Sometimes someone even says something that in another's version of Spanish is offensive or even lewd—in which case we are momentarily shocked, then smile and move on. In those churches, not all the music represents our own taste, but we have learned to live and to worship together because, after all, we are family. In Catholic Hispanic churches, the sense of mystery at the Eucharist is heightened, rather than lessened. In Latino Pentecostal churches, and in many others, it is not unusual for someone to speak in "tongues." In that case, if there is someone to interpret, it is done; but if there is no such person available, the unintelligible words are still considered part of the worship of God.

It is for all of these reasons that I said at the beginning of this essay that perhaps it is in our very multiplicity—in the impossibility of defining and describing us as a whole—that our greatest contribution to the worship of the church at large lies. We have learned how to worship together, even though we are not all alike. We have learned how to worship together in congregations in which people come from radically different strata of society, where some speak mostly English and very little Spanish, while others know mostly Spanish and very little English, and where there are several different variants of Span-ish spoken. We have learned to worship and celebrate together even across significant theological lines. We have learned how to do this by combining a spirit of fiesta with a profound sense of mystery. The fiesta makes us all participants, and thus leads to the mystery of transgenerational, transclass, and transcultural communication. The mystery reminds us of the otherness of God, and thus makes it possible for all to celebrate the glory of one another's otherness. In mystery and awe we celebrate the fiesta, until the final veil shall be

removed, and in fiesta we shall all worship together the ever-
lasting mystery of God. It is our prayer and our hope that the
rest of God's family—including our monolingual English-
speaking sisters, brothers, and cousins—may share in the same
mystery and the same joy!

CHAPTER TWO

Allan Figueroa Deck, S.J.

# Hispanic Catholic Prayer and Worship

The reality of prayer and worship among Roman Catholics and Protestants of Latin American origin is a generally unexplored topic. Relatively little has been written about it, although recent publications in the area of U.S. Hispanic/Latino theology are beginning to fill a great void.[1] This is actually an extremely important and revelatory subject, for it is precisely in prayer and worship, as opposed to other areas of religious practice and theological theory, that Hispanics, whether Roman Catholic or Protestant, express the complexity, richness, and stunning originality of their particular religious heritage.[2]

Much of what is most distinctive in the religious heritage of Hispanic Americans is expressed in the vast gamut of symbols, rituals, and stories around which their life of prayer and worship revolves. Powerful symbols rooted in the Bible and in Catholic tradition have taken on new life as they combine with the equally powerful symbols of the indigenous and African cultures first evangelized by the Spaniards five hundred years ago.[3] Hispanic exposure to powerful Protestant preaching that makes otherwise dead biblical images and stories come alive has added to the already vivid historical Catholic religious imagination.

The traditional prayer and worship of Hispanic Roman Catholics is permeated with a symbolic, sacramental imagination that continues its influence even as these people migrate and experience "the acids of modernity." To understand their forms and styles of worship and prayer is to come close to their particular form of Catholic Christianity as well as to their culture.[4] This discussion of popular Hispanic religiosity may also shed light on Hispanic Protestantism.

The tenacity with which the Latin American masses have maintained their traditional Catholic identity even in the face of ongoing criticism from their official teachers (bishops, priests, catechists, religious) is remarkable. They have also often resisted the active proselytism of some Protestant missioners who had little understanding of and sympathy for the relationship between popular Catholic customs and the cultural identity of the people. The vast majority of Hispanic Americans became and have remained Catholics despite the serious abuses of the institutional Catholic Church (for example, the Church's historical identification with oppressive colonial power) and the absence and/or unworthiness of their own official ministers, that is, the priests. This Catholic form of Christianity, however, exists in the form of popular religion and survives in many secondary forms, as Segundo Galilea tells us, in the context of the people's migrations to urban centers and across international borders.[5] While losing much of its previous vigor and rootedness in the millennial rural existence of the Latin American masses, popular Catholicism in these modern times is alive and well even though, at times, it is under considerable duress. Hispanic popular Catholicism is not a negligible phenomenon.

Indeed, researchers are noting the tendency of Hispanic Protestants who ostensibly have broken with the Catholic sacramentals and rituals to "revert" to certain features of Hispanic Catholic piety. One of these has to do with elements surrounding the baptism of infants. Another is devotion to the Virgin Mary, especially under her title of Guadalupe, reflected in the presence of her image even in some Protestant churches! A third is the custom of requesting *los santos óleos,* the sacrament of the sick, from a priest.[6]

One really cannot know Hispanic Catholicism by studying official, formal, or normative Roman Catholicism. Rather, one must confront Hispanic popular Catholicism, which is a constellation of celebrations, rites, graphic symbols, and underlying values that revolve around prayer and worship of a transcendent God mediated through all of creation.

I wish to spotlight this aspect of Hispanic Catholic religious heritage—its prayer and worship—first, by providing a context for discussing this topic; second, by describing what is meant by Hispanic Catholic prayer and worship and showing how a popular Protestantism similar in several ways to Hispanic Catholicism also exists; and third, by suggesting some implications for Hispanic ministry and ecumenical relations with Hispanic Protestants, especially evangelicals and Pentecostals.

## Contextualizing the Issue

Hispanic theologians take for granted the fact that one of the salient characteristics of U.S. Hispanic/Latino theology, both Roman Catholic and Protestant, is its relative newness. Almost one-third of worldwide Roman Catholicism is made up of people of Hispanic origin, living particularly in Latin America and the United States. The most dynamic parts of many Protestant denominations in the United States, both historical mainline and evangelical, are Hispanic and Asian. Yet these Catholics and Protestants have generally remained on the margin with respect to the Spanish and European Church, and also in the United States, with respect to the mainline English-speaking hierarchies or judicatories. Only recently have Hispanic Catholics or Protestants begun to produce their own writers, intellectuals, and theologians.[7] The majority of these Hispanics, especially in Latin America, are rural peasants and urban factory and service workers. They neither enjoy the leisure nor have the formal education needed to articulate their experiences. Since these people are poor and uneducated, their particular forms of prayer and worship—their brands of Catholic or evangelical Christianity—have been disdained as inferior, superstitious, and anomalous.

Interestingly enough, *both* official Catholic teachers such as bishops, priests, and theologians *and* Protestant missioners and theologians have long looked down on the religion of the people. Harvey Cox pointed this out a few years ago in his book *Religion in the Secular City.*[8] Cox was reflecting on the discovery of hidden power and resources in the religion of ordinary people. He notes that official leaders have tended to dismiss the people's religion. Catholic priests have tended to apologize for what they believe was an inadequate, often superficial assimilation of true, orthodox Christian beliefs on the part of the Indians and consequently of the masses. Protestants have insisted even more on the lack of true Christian belief on the part of the popular Catholic Masses. Protestant writers have pointed to the limited view of Jesus Christ, the emphasis on the "dead Jesus" characteristic of so much popular Catholic devotion.[9] These commentators also believe that the strong emphasis on the Virgin Mary reflects a distorted and ultimately inadequate view of redemption that fails to acknowledge Jesus Christ as personal Savior. Cox, however, maintains that this dismissal of popular religion is a mistake. He points to three significant facts: first, the rise of a strong evangelical Pentecostal movement, a "popular" form of Protestant Christianity; second, the sometimes heroic activities of Catholic base Christian communities of poor and oppressed peoples; and, third, the extraordinary persistence of devotion to the Virgin Mary under her distinct titles but especially as the Virgin of Guadalupe and the hidden *liberative* power for both men and women of this resistant and powerful symbol.[10]

Recent writings by Latin Americans stress the insight of the Italian Marxist Antonio Gramsci who parted with his fellow Marxists in his interpretation of the subaltern social class. He believed that the religion of the poor, of the masses—in his experience, the popular Catholicism of the South of Italy—was a powerful expression of resistance to historical oppression. This religiosity therefore plays an important part in the process of transformative action or revolution and should not be disdained as an opiate in classic Marxist fashion.[11] Gramsci saw that the vivid religious imagery of the poor was a basic ingredient in their empowerment, a source of motivation in their struggle for survival. Perhaps it could be channeled in such a way as to promote real, radical social change and not remain purely symbolic.

Despite these positive views regarding people's religion from thinkers like Gramsci, Cox, and others, the context for discussing Hispanic popular Catholicism and Protestantism is still predominantly a negative one. Cox decries this because he has come to see that the people's religion is a special instance of *resistance* to oppression on the part of the native peoples and their progeny in the New World. It is also a provider of profound and valid insight about the mystery of God and the supernatural. Evangelical Protestant writer Tito Paredes expresses this idea:

> Societies where popular religiosity is predominant are closer to the worldview of the Bible in the sense that the Bible gives equal

importance both to the supernatural and natural world. The spiritual
dimension of humans is recognized both by the Bible and by the
popular religious sectors.[12]

The worldview of uneducated *campesinos* and urban factory
workers often resembles the world of the Bible, its views and
values, better than that of today's secularized Catholics and
Protestants alike. While there are important elements of the
Christian message that have yet to permeate the people's
religion, there are important truths about God and perhaps
even about Jesus Christ that popular religiosity may actually
convey to both Roman Catholic and Protestant elites alike.
*Both* of these major Christian traditions have exhibited a drive
toward domination, imposition, and proselytism over the
centuries.

### Describing Popular Hispanic Catholicism

Popular Hispanic Catholicism is exuberantly sacramental;
that is, it affirms the ability of created things to draw us to the
Creator, and of the Creator to draw close to us *through* these
things (water, bread, wine, spoken words, gestures, signs,
images, incense, and so on). This expression of Christian faith
is propagated through oral communication and performance,
not through literal biblical texts. It is not based on the Bible in
the sense that it is a preliterate, pre-Reformation form of
Christianity that tends to relate to the images, symbols, and
stories of the Bible in a fluid, often indirect manner, not
specifically and intentionally as is the case in a literate Christian
community with easy access to the printed Word of God.
Hispanic popular Catholicism is also a particularly strong
example of a kind of religious imagination that works through
analogy as opposed to one that works dialectically. What I
mean by this is that Hispanic popular culture does not relate
to life's search for meaning by seeking for some overarching
coherence to be achieved by ultimately getting rid of inconsis-

tencies. Nor does it find much consolation in conceptualizations or abstract principles or in most forms of contemporary theology. Rather, the underlying concept of truth is layered in such a way that things can be the *same* in some ways (consistent) but *different* in others (inconsistent). Such tension is viewed positively. Real and/or seemingly competing truths at various levels of life and reality are simply *held in tension*. Inconsistencies do not always need to be resolved. Often they must be lived with. This is manifested in the popular Hispanic fascination with mystery. And is not our faith ultimately a mystery? Modern European (especially Nordic), American, and Protestant cultures have stressed a dialectical religious imagination; that is, they have systematically sought to eliminate inconsistencies on behalf of a literate, logical, and rational view of the Christian heritage.

Many modern Protestant and Catholic theologies have been driven by a desire to achieve "scientific" legitimacy. In the face of this drive, Hispanic Catholicism, being premodern, traditional, and steeped in popular myth, symbol, and ritual, seems atavistic, a throwback to the abuses and superstitions of the Middle Ages. To mainline Protestants, evangelical and especially Pentecostal Christianity appears in a similar unflattering light. Because the people's religion stresses symbol rather than an articulate, cognitive knowledge of the faith, this religiosity tends to be open-ended. By their very nature symbols and biblical imagery are open to diverse interpretation, whereas literal texts are much more confining.

In addition, Hispanic Catholicism stresses the senses. The prayer and worship of Hispanic Catholics involves the whole body. For instance, there are smells associated with incense (used traditionally in Roman Catholicism and in Native American religions), sounds such as bells, many kinds of popular songs or hymns, diverse bodily postures such as kneeling, standing, and sitting. Historically there have been bodily penances such as walking on one's knees, long pilgrimages on

foot, scourging with a small whip (flagellation), and the carrying of crosses in imitation of Christ.

Visually, Hispanic Catholicism provides a feast for the eyes.
Lavish artwork, brilliant colors, sensual curves, intricate designs, abundant flowers, and many flickering candles are ordinary embellishments for the people's prayer and worship. The
spirit of the Spanish baroque was enhanced and deepened by
the Indian renderings of Spanish designs.

The baroque sensibility became deeply ingrained in Hispanic Catholics. This includes the visual and sensual aspects
but goes beyond them to include a profound sense of drama.
This is exemplified most clearly at the major feasts. At Christ-
mastime there are *posadas* and *pastorelas,* popular dramatizations of the infancy narratives in the Gospels. During Holy
Week there is the *Via Crucis,* the Way of the Cross. In these
dramatizations the actors are the faithful themselves, not pro-
fessionals. These aspects of Hispanic popular piety are most
visible during Holy Week in countless towns throughout Latin
America and in places like Seville in Spain. These characteristics of popular Hispanic Catholicism are undoubtedly
rooted in the medieval and baroque practices of Spain, but also
in very similar tendencies in native American and African
religions with which Hispanic popular Catholicism seems to
be in a kind of *permanent* dialogue.[13]

One of the effects of this particular style of prayer and
worship is its strong appeal to the imagination. The popular
prayer of Hispanic Catholics is nourished by many aids to the
imagination and as such reflects a spirit of contemplation
whereby the entire person is brought into dialogue with God
by the use of the senses as well as the mind. Hispanic Catholicism flees from abstract approaches to God and prefers the
concrete.

Another good example of this is the enduring popularity of
the rosary. This is an ancient form of prayer brought from Asia
to Christian Europe in the Middle Ages. It is a simple but

effective way to pray, especially for people who are not literate or only marginally literate. The verbal content is a biblically inspired prayer based on the angel's salutation to Mary in Luke's Gospel.

Related to the *sensuality* of Hispanic Catholic prayer and worship is its *somatic* character, that is, its tendency to involve the body in prayer. This is seen in the place given to dance. Examples of this are found in the *matachin* dances that adorn the more important feast days such as Christmas, Easter, Corpus Christi, or the feast of the town's patron saint. Similarly, Hispanic popular Catholicism, which is rooted in the lives of Africans and mulattos in the Caribbean and the coasts of Mexico, Central America, and South America has incorporated dance within the context of the larger celebration, not usually in church but either before or after the church service.

Popular Hispanic Catholicism, because of its symbolic richness and sensuality, is therefore more akin to Eastern Catholicism or Orthodoxy than it is to either Western Roman Catholicism (which was always rather austere in its approach to worship and ritual) or to Protestantism. In this connection the extraordinary importance of the Virgin Mary as mother of Jesus and "feminine face of God" in Hispanic Catholicism is quite reminiscent of the Eastern Orthodox tradition.

The traditional forms of Hispanic Catholic prayer and worship are distributed throughout the liturgical year. Certainly, Christmas and Holy Week provide a series of engaging events that celebrate God's saving action in history through Jesus Christ. In addition to the Church's official liturgy (the Eucharist, the seven sacraments, and the service of biblical readings, chants, and excerpts from early Christian writers called the Liturgy of the Hours) Hispanic American Catholics have developed their own popular forms of celebration. The *pastorela* or shepherd's play was brought to Latin America by the first missionaries. It is a form of the *auto sacramental,* the medieval mystery play commemorating events in the life of

Jesus Christ. The *pastorela* is traditionally presented in the days before Christmas around the time of the *posadas*. The *posadas* reenact Mary's and Joseph's search for an inn on the night of Jesus' birth as recorded in the Gospels. The *posadas* combine prayerful reflection on the biblical passage, special songs, a ritual procession, knocking on several doors, and finally the jubilant opening of the door to the wayfaring Holy Family. The *posada* ends with a party for the children of the neighborhood and the breaking of the *piñata*. The *posada*, to the delight of the children, is repeated for nine consecutive evenings culminating in the *gran posada* of Christmas Eve.

There are other ceremonies, many of them taking place at home and not at church, that induce the Hispanic faithful to prayer centered on salvation history. There is the moment when an image of the Baby Jesus is laid down in the manger on Christmas Eve. Special prayers are said. The image is provided with special dress. The entire family as well as friends and neighbors are invited to this traditional event. Special food is served at the conclusion.

Traditionally, the day for exchanging gifts is not Christmas but the Feast of the Epiphany. On that day, known as *el Día de los Reyes,* the community gathers (again, usually at home, not at the church) to share the *rosca,* a cake made in the form of a crown or wreath. A small image of the child Jesus is hidden in the cake, and the person who receives the image in his or her cake is supposed to prepare the party the following year.

Holy Week is another high point for the popular religion of Hispanics. The Way of the Cross or *Via Crucis* is presented by the faithful themselves who assume the various roles in the drama of Jesus' passion. Participants wear realistic costumes, and it is not uncommon for the person playing the role of Jesus to appear literally crucified. Of course, he is not nailed to a cross! He is attached in such a way that it looks as if he is being nailed, and fake blood is sometimes used. These dramatizations are done with profound seriousness. They are extremely moving because they manifest the degree to which ordinary Hispanic Catholics have identified with the person and passion of Jesus Christ—even though oftentimes, it is true, they have not explicitly accepted him as their personal Savior.

Puerto Rican Catholics have the custom of the *encuentro* in which they reenact the meeting of Jesus with his mother after the Resurrection. Mexican Catholics have the Good Friday custom of *el pésame,* a dramatic sermon in which the preacher dialogues with Mary about the events leading to Jesus' crucifixion.

One of the remarkable characteristics of Hispanic popular devotion is its resistance to being confined to services in church. In this regard, Hispanic Catholicism reflects its premodern, rural roots. The worship of God cannot be limited to discrete times, to an hour or so, in church. Rather, the sense of *celebration* logically permeates an entire day, several days, or in the example of Holy Week in Seville, a whole week! The worship of God is not limited to what happens in church. Nor is it only what happens in an individual's heart. It is *par excellence* what the *community,* the Body of Christ, does. Worship and prayer are concerned with the entire feast, the music, the party, the dance, and most certainly the food. All of these are ways in which saving moments in the life of Christ and his people are celebrated.

The indigenous peoples of the Americas and Africans have contributed to Hispanic Catholicism an enduring conviction about dance as a true form of prayer. In both official Roman Catholicism and Protestantism such an idea is problematic. European and Anglo American Catholics have been imbued with a strain of Augustinianism that makes them uncomfortable with the sensual aspects of human existence. Protestants, perhaps for similar reasons, or because they interpret certain biblical injunctions in a particular way, have great difficulty in admitting dance as a form of prayer. Many cultures, however, do admit dance as a form of communion with God. Popular

Hispanic Catholicism is somewhat open to this proposition and manifests it at the time of fiesta.

**Implications**

One of the underlying implications of this reflection on popular Hispanic Catholic prayer and worship is the strong relationship between Latin American culture and religious sensibility. Neither official Roman Catholicism nor Protestantism has been able to erase some of the deep-seated cultural orientations of Hispanics. These orientations are rooted in the complex process of inculturation that took place centuries ago that created the *mestizo* cultures of the Americas. Popular Protestantism in its evangelical and Pentecostal forms also manifests many of these same qualities. Consequently, Roman Catholic and Protestant Hispanics may have more in common upon which to dialogue than has generally been acknowledged.

Pentecostalism is thriving among Hispanics perhaps more than any other cultural group in the world. Why is that? Perhaps it has to do with the *continuity* between the ancient expressions of popular Latin American Catholicism and contemporary Pentecostalism: strong affirmation of a transcendent God, small community context for prayer, emphasis on God's miraculous power, openness to mystery, orientation to healing of every kind (physical, psychological, social), and affective appeal to the working class and the poor based on the strong use of symbolism, imagery, ritual, and story (biblically and/or sacramentally based).[14]

In recent years both Protestant and Roman Catholic thinkers, especially missiologists, have insisted on the need for contextualization and inculturation of the faith. When one approaches the subject of prayer and worship from the point of view of cultural anthropology, and not from that of official teachers and theologians, one can discern several constants, several similarities in the spontaneous manner in which Catholic and Protestant Hispanics approach God. While one cannot belittle the reality of doctrinal differences, it becomes clear that at a deeper level Hispanics tend to relate to God, to pray, to "seek the face of God" through vivid imagery of a sacramental and/or biblical nature and in a manner that is profoundly affective.[15] If one adds to that the similar social realities—struggle, marginalization, and injustice—that Catholic as well as Protestant Hispanics experience, there is reason to say that a new and promising search for Christian unity may be in the making.

# CHAPTER THREE

Samuel Solíván

# Hispanic Pentecostal Worship

The Pentecostal movement is among the youngest of North American–bred religious phenomena, the product of the 1906 Azusa Street revival, led by an African American named James W. Seymour and supported by a multiracial, multiethnic congregation. This Holy Spirit revival has spread throughout the world. David Martin, a British sociologist, writes in his book *Tongues of Fire* about the phenomenal growth of this movement in Latin America and other Third World countries. He characterizes this movement as the first modern popular Protestant movement.[1]

The Pentecostal movement is comprised of a growing number of independent local and international organizations that

Hispanics or Latinos call *concilios* (councils). The largest of these is the Assemblies of God. By some estimates Pentecostals number 350 million plus worldwide, and the numbers are still growing rapidly. In some countries in Latin America, Pentecostal growth surpasses or is quickly approaching the national population growth rate.[2] As noted by David Martin, Pentecostals will soon outnumber Roman Catholics in some Latin American countries.[3]

Similar growth among North American Hispanics is also evident. For instance, in the Assemblies of God, Hispanics represent the growing constituency of that denomination. Hispanic Americans today constitute 22 to 25 percent of the membership of the Assemblies of God. It should also be noted that there are several exclusively Hispanic Pentecostal *concilios,* such as Assemblies of Christian Churches, Iglesia de Dios Pentecostal Misión Internacional, Movimiento Iglesia Pentecostal Internacional, Iglesias Damasco, and many others.

Pentecostalism encompasses a number of different theological and historical streams. There are several types, or schools, of Pentecostals, including Trinitarian, Oneness Apostolic Pentecostals, classical and neoclassical Pentecostals. The Assemblies represent the mainstream of Trinitarian Pentecostalism and the Apostolic Faith Pentecostals represent the Oneness tradition. All Pentecostals emphasize the Baptism of the Holy Spirit as evidenced by speaking in tongues, along with healing, and the return (*parousia*) of the Lord.[4]

Yet between North American English-speaking Pentecostals and Latino Pentecostals there are some noticeable differences. The remainder of this paper will identify and comment on these differences. It should also be noted that Hispanic/Latino Pentecostals are not monolithic—nor is the Latino community in the United States. There are a variety of Hispanic American communities in the United States. Mexican-Americans comprise the largest segment. Puerto Ricans and Cubans follow. Central and South Americans as well as Spaniards make up the rest of the Hispanic American community. Each national Hispanic group has introduced to its Pentecostal expression its own *sazón,* or flavor. Depending on the place of origin of the pastor and the majority of the congregation, a Pentecostal worship service will vary. Yet a number of things are common to most Hispanic Pentecostal congregations. I would note that a practice that is uncommon among most Pentecostals yet present among the Church of God (Mission Board) congregations is ritual foot washing.[5]

It can be said that worship and evangelism lie at the very center of the life of the Pentecostal community. An examination of Pentecostal worship is the lens through which one can best see and understand Pentecostalism. Pentecostalism is more than a directory of theological or doctrinal statements or the experience of speaking in tongues. It is more than a list of "do's" and "don'ts." Pentecostals are best understood in the context of worship and its relation to evangelism and mission. These aspects lie at the very heart of the community's self-understanding. Pentecostals are a community with an evangelistic mission.

## The Locus of Pentecostal Worship

Probably the most immediate difference when comparing Hispanic Pentecostal worship with other expressions of Christian worship is the location and context within which Pentecostal worship commonly occurs. Whereas most mainline Protestant churches are located in the suburbs or at the periphery of urban centers, most Hispanic Pentecostal churches are located in the poorest of the urban barrios. Whereas mainline churches worship in buildings intentionally designed for Christian worship, most Hispanic Pentecostal churches worship in storefronts, or in other buildings rehabilitated for use as a place of worship. A growing number of Pentecostal congregations meet in the underutilized facilities of mainline churches in need of income.

The location of the church is usually the first level of resistance or difference for non-Pentecostals in trying to understand Hispanic Pentecostalism, for it relocates them to a social space they have worked hard at leaving behind. Not only will the worship experience be different; already the social location is different and at times even intimidating or frightening. The location of Pentecostal churches is not accidental. They are located where the largest portion of the Hispanic community lives. Latinos in the United States are primarily located in the major urban centers and are among the poorest in the country. Like much of the apostolic church, we too are an urban church.

Storefronts and other buildings are renovated into places of worship. The architecture and the ornaments in the church are not those usually found in church buildings. Homemade altars and pulpits are common. Lighting fixtures are commonly replaced by kitchen chandeliers, and other trappings by more commonly available furniture. Often the discarded benches of mainline churches that are moving out of the area or that have closed are recycled for use in our churches. The windows are covered with homemade curtains. Instead of expensively woven tapestries and altar linens, one sees handmade knitted or crocheted pulpit covers. The furniture and other trappings in the church reflect the culture and economic reality of the congregation. The color schemes often reflect the art of their countries of origin. Lively colors such as yellow, blue, and red contrast with the solemn color schemes present in mainline churches. Stained-glass windows are not Tiffany glass, but plastic stick-on imitations.

The location in the barrio is also indicative of the ecclesiology of many of our churches. The church is understood as being called to serve the local community. The church's membership is comprised mostly of people living in the immediate vicinity, within walking distance or within easily accessible public transportation. Pentecostal churches are to a great extent prototypes of *comunidades de base* (base communities) made famous by Latin American Liberation theologians. This fact is important insofar as the churches minister to a community of which they are a part, to people who they know, and by whom the church is known. The members of the church share with others in their community their common lot and are personally acquainted with one another's needs.

The location of Hispanic Pentecostal churches also speaks of the type of ministry and people they are committed to reach with the gospel. Orlando Costas, a respected Puerto Rican missiologist, wrote that these are those "outside the gate": the forgotten, dispossessed, marginalized, and unattended people of our society.[6] The church reaches out to those who have few resources for responding to the daily challenges of life. It is the church that stands in the midst of life's storms and reaches out to those in need of refuge. It is the church of the Galileans, the Samaritans of our times, a church of the poor, as Costas argues. This is in contrast to the upwardly mobile, quickly growing middle-class composition of Anglo Pentecostalism, as in the case of the Assemblies of God.

The socioeconomic reality of the Hispanic community and the location of the Hispanic Pentecostal church also reflect its worldview. Often Hispanic Pentecostals understand themselves to be a bulwark against death and the forces of evil that are overwhelming the world. They are a fortress against the cultural forces that seek to destroy them and their value system—a system that they understand as reflecting the values of the Kingdom of God and their Lord Jesus Christ. This countercultural posture is the counterpart of the attitude that the dominant culture has had and continues to have toward them. This worldview plays an important part in the ethos of their worship, which is fueled by an eschatological—at times even apocalyptic—vision of the future.

After overcoming the fears of going to the barrio to worship with Latino Pentecostals, one is faced with a world of difference. Whereas in mainline churches one is part of a community that is often homogeneous, Hispanic churches introduce one to a community of color. Hispanic people are in Virgilio Elizondo's words a *mestizo* people.[7] We are a people with a cultural and racial heritage that embraces the total spectrum of color and of several races. The physical features of indigenous Native Americans, Blacks, and White Europeans are all represented among Hispanic Americans. The Mexican writer José Vasconcelos spoke of this *mestizaje* as "la Raza Cósmica," the cosmic race.[8]

The fact that we are a *mestizo* people (the *mestizaje* varying in its composition in relation to geographical location) is also reflected in our worship, in our songs, music, leadership, and liturgical styles. We understand our diversity to be a gift of God and representative of what Christ seeks the whole church to be: diverse yet one.

This racial and culture diversity presents us with the challenge of fashioning a liturgical style that is flexible and capable of responding to the diversity present among us. This leads us to consider the "liturgical style" or manner of Pentecostal worship.

**Pentecostal Worship—Liturgy** [9]

In most Pentecostal churches formal liturgy is almost nonexistent. Yet a liturgy is discernible by those who are better acquainted with Pentecostal worship. As a nonconfessional, nonliturgical tradition, Pentecostal worship is not constrained by the confessions of the church or by the history of its liturgy. The gathered community is free to be led by the Holy Spirit within the guidelines of scripture, its own worship tradition (liturgy), and the culture and language of the community.

Three important elements inform Pentecostal liturgy and contribute to the church's ability to contextualize its worship. The first of these theological presuppositions is the priesthood of all believers; second, its noncreedal tradition; and third, its nonliturgical orientation.

*Priesthood of All Believers—Ministry of the Laity*

An appreciation of the priesthood of all believers (laymen and laywomen, as well as clergy, children, young adults, and the elderly) provides the entire congregation with an opportunity to play a role in the worship of the community. This is not to deny that among some Pentecostal groups the role of women continues in an official or unofficial sense to be subject to the discretion of male clergy.

Nevertheless, women and men, as well as young adults and children, provide leadership in various aspects of worship. This participation is fostered and encouraged through the activities of children's and youth societies that meet weekly during the year. These different societies provide a small group setting for teaching and modeling church leadership. In these societal meetings, the worship services are planned and implemented by their members. Children learn to speak in public, give their testimonies, and lead in congregational singing, preaching, and praying. It is in these smaller societal meetings that worship leadership is practiced and nurtured among the young and the laity.

In these smaller group services the community identifies, encourages, and nurtures the diverse gifts and ministries of the Holy Spirit present among its members. The leadership developed at this level serves as a resource pool for the major worship services during the week. It is common among most Hispanic Pentecostals to find a young adult leading the devotional part of worship, while younger children are encouraged to sing, recite from memory verses of scripture, or even lead in public prayer. Age, gender, and color are secondary concerns. What is most important is the leading of the Holy Spirit and the affirmation of a person's ministry and/or gifts, and the use of these gifts for the edification of the congregation.

*Noncreedal Stance*

A second important aspect of Hispanic Pentecostal worship is its noncreedal stance. Pentecostals in general, and Hispanic Pentecostals in particular, do not feel accountable to being defined by any church confession, or ecumenical creed. Their sole basis of authority for informing worship is scripture as interpreted and applied by the community.

This noncreedalism frees worship style to be defined by the context and culture of the community. It frees it from being defined by creedal statements or theological interpretations of the church's confessions or its ecumenical creeds. It is not a denial of the content of the confessions and creeds of the church generally recognized by the Reformed Protestant tradition. Rather, it is a relocation of the people's place and function in the life of the community. Pentecostals do affirm the Apostles' Creed and the Nicene Creed among others. But the creeds do not define or constrain the content and nature of worship. This stance is an affirmation of the singular authority of Scripture, and the freedom of the Spirit to lead the church today in its worship in a similar manner to that of the apostolic church.

This understanding of creeds and confessions reflects the absence of formal training in the movement. Theology as human discourse about God, Christ, and the Holy Spirit, as well as other beliefs held by our fellowship, functions at an informal, popular level of reflection and usually not at the formal level of critical theological reflection often present in the mainline churches. Again I note that this does not mean that there is an absence of theology or liturgy. Rather, their shape and form are different from traditional approaches. An informed rehearsal of Pentecostal doctrine will quickly reveal its deep and serious dependence on its Wesleyan, Arminian, and Reformed heritage, as well as the influence of the radical wing of the Reformation.

## *Nonliturgical Tradition*

A third aspect of Hispanic Pentecostal worship is its nonliturgical tradition. This is not a claim that Pentecostal worship has no rhyme or reason theologically. Hispanic Pentecostal worship does possess and follow a liturgical structure or logic. Yet this liturgical structure is informal and unwritten, and becomes obvious to the regular attendee at worship. It is nonliturgical in that it does not necessarily have to follow the ritualistic sequence often assumed in most mainline churches. It is nonliturgical in that no one is instructed formally to follow a predetermined order of worship established by someone outside of the community. It is nonliturgical in the sense that there is no single correct or normative pattern for conducting worship.

A liturgy is present in that there is an intentional theology that informs the progress of the service. Yet there is flexibility in that the untrained layperson is not asked to follow a specifically prepared ritual in leading the community in worship. Usually laypersons are the ones who lead the community in worship and are free to lead as they feel led to by the Spirit and on the basis of the tradition of worship they have observed in their congregations and in other Pentecostal Hispanic congregations. This "open liturgy" or "free liturgy" lends itself for incorporating into the service the particularity of the community and its cultural expressions.

Four general principles can be said to inform this "open liturgy": an openness to the leading of the Holy Spirit; an environment of expectation that the Holy Spirit will meet us as we worship; an openness to be free to praise God and God's Word as it addresses us in worship; and passionate and participatory worship. Within these rubrics an "open liturgy" is free to evolve.

**Components of Hispanic Pentecostal Worship**

*Prayers*

Among some congregations a set pattern of worship is clearly evident. This, in fact, becomes the liturgy. Some of the parts of worship present in most Hispanic Pentecostal services are prayers of various types; invocations; thanksgiving prayers for healing; prayers of praise and adoration; and intercessory pastoral and lay prayers.

*The Reading of Scripture, Old and New Testaments*

Rarely is one scripture reading given more authority than another as is the case in some mainline traditions such as the Episcopal and Roman Catholic, where the reading of the Gospels is treated with greater respect than other readings from the Psalms or the Epistles—as expressed, for instance, in having to stand while the Gospel selection is read. The entire Scriptures are seen to be the Word of the Lord and as such the congregation is often asked to stand during the reading of any scripture.

*Coritos (Hymnody)*

Singing is an ever present and important part of the worship service. The singing is carried on primarily by the congregation, at times by a soloist or other groups. Hymns, spiritual songs, psalms and other scripture portions are sung in the form of *coritos*. These are usually short and repetitive spiritual songs that often tell a story, but always include praise—usually a psalm or other portion of scripture. The *corito* is an indigenous Hispanic Pentecostal singing style. The praising of the Lord and the testimony of the community are expressed in song at a variety of places in the service. These *coritos* or popular songs can sometimes be found in a songbook or in a chorus book prepared by the local congregation, but most often they are memorized. Of the homemade *coritarios,* or collections of *coritos,* very few provide music, as this too is part of the oral tradition of the church. Also, beyond these *coritos,* Hispanic Pentecostals use more traditional hymnbooks. The most popular of these is *Himnos de gloria y triunfo.*[10]

*Testimonios (Testimonies)*

Another important part of the community's worship service is the *testimonios.* During most services the congregation is asked if anyone has a word of testimony to the love and mercy of the Lord. Testimonies of healing, economic provision, and expressions of thanksgiving for answered prayers and mercies are shared with the congregation. This is the place in the community's life in worship where both the burdens of the congregation and the joy of answered prayer are shared with others as all seek congregational support in the form of prayers. This time of testimony is also the place where one gains insight into the common and daily struggles of the community and the concrete ways God has answered their prayers. Testimony time is a public witness to the ongoing ministry of the Holy Spirit in the life of the community. It engenders faith, thanksgiving, and hope. It also serves to keep the community abreast of the needs, concerns, and celebrations of its members.

*El Mensaje (The Message—Preaching)*

Probably the most important part of the service is the preaching of the Word, usually by the pastor or other church leader, male or female. On Sundays the pastor or an invited guest preacher, usually an evangelist, is normally responsible for the sermon. At times, local lay leaders who have demonstrated a gift for preaching are asked to sharpen their preaching gifts during weeknight services, which often take place three or four evenings a week. In most Hispanic Pentecostal churches, the preaching of the gospel is open to men and women, lay and ordained. What is required is the community's affirmation that one should possess a preaching gift and preach with "anointing"—that is, with clear signs that one is led by the Holy Spirit. The preacher in the Hispanic Pentecostal tradition sees himself/herself as a messenger from God with a word for the people of God. Preaching is understood to be in the tradition of the Old Testament prophets who, inspired by an encounter with God, brought the Word of the Lord to the people. The typical message lasts at least forty-five minutes—on special occasions at least an hour to an hour and a half. Brief messages are rare. The people come to worship expecting to spend at least two to three hours, especially on Sundays.

It should also be pointed out that in most Hispanic Pentecostal churches the most important worship service is held on Sunday evenings. This is what is often called the evangelistic service (*servicio evangelístico*). Its principal focus is "soul-winning." This is to be contrasted with the midweek services, whose aim is more the edification of the congregation and the celebration of God's love. The principal purpose of the message is to introduce and challenge non-Christians present to accept Christ as their personal Savior. The "altar call" and "altar service" are the climax of the evangelistic service. This is an invitation to non-Christians to come forward to accept Christ as their Savior, followed by a time of prayer, intercession, and thanksgiving at the altar.

A hymn or a *corito* of thanksgiving and praise followed by a benediction by the pastor or someone else in the congregation serves to bring the service to a close.

**Pentecostal Ethos: Passionate Worship**

The liturgical traditions among English-speaking Protestant churches in the United States run from High Church to various expressions of working-class nonliturgical worship. To a great extent, what is most common among them is the absence of passion in worship. This attention to reverential formality is often a vehicle for managing the passion-impairment of American Anglo European culture. Worship is often understood as a private nonpassionate occasion, mostly cognitively oriented.

In this there is a contrast, not only between mainline Christians and Pentecostals in the dominant culture, but even more so between Anglo and Hispanic Pentecostals. The expression of passion is not only a matter of degree among Hispanic Pentecostals; passion is a constituent makeup of Hispanic culture. Most that we do is done with enthusiasm, whether it be socializing, working, or praising God.

Passionately and unapologetically, Hispanic Pentecostal worship expresses the profound experience of conversion the community has known both personally and collectively. Faith in Christ, Christian discipleship, is understood to be more than a cognitive matter. It is a personal relationship of love between the believer and Christ, empowered by the Holy Spirit.

Often in the midst of the worship service, and at various times, persons led by the Holy Spirit address the worshiping community with a word of prophecy (typically a biblical exhortation), or share a message in tongues, often interpreted by some other member of the congregation. These messages in tongues are often messages of encouragement or rebuke, or calls for reconciliation, faithfulness, or praise. Among most Pentecostal communities there is an accepted order for these expressions of charismata. Central to Pentecostal worship is the expectation that the Holy Spirit will make herself known among the people at worship. It is the presence of the charismata in the life of the congregation in worship and in mission that characterizes Pentecostal Christianity. The fruit and gifts of the Spirit are expected to be evident in the daily life and mission of the church. It is the Holy Spirit who empowers the church for its evangelistic mission in the world.

Like other Christian communities, the Pentecostal Hispanic church seeks to be faithful to Christ's mandate to evangelize the world—to proclaim the gospel, "the good news" in bad times that Christ so loved the world that he gave himself for it.

The Pentecostal community in general, and the Hispanic Pentecostal community in particular, await the blessed hope of the church—Christ's return. It is this hope that provides the fervor and urgency of its message. Maranatha! Come, Lord Jesus!

CHAPTER FOUR

María Luisa Santillán Baert

# Worship in the Hispanic United Methodist Church

Cantemos al Señor un himno de alegría.
¡Aleluya! ¡Aleluya! Cantemos al Señor. ¡Aleluya!
(Let's sing unto the Lord a hymn of glad rejoicing.
Alleluia! Alleluia! Let's sing unto the Lord. Alleluia!)

Thus reads in part the first stanza of one of the eighteen Spanish language hymns composed by Hispanics and included in *The United Methodist Hymnal.* An English translation is given beside the Spanish words to enable non-Spanish speakers to participate in the faith expression of thought and rhythm of Hispanics. For the first time *The United*

*57*

*Methodist Hymnal* (1989 edition) includes worship resources from its multicultural and pluralistic constituency.

Religion, faith, culture, and life are inseparable for Latinos. Almost from birth Hispanics know that there is a mighty and loving God. As the Hispanic infant is nurtured physically and spiritually, emotionally and mentally, the child hears God's name in everyday conversation, and thus becomes familiar with it. A relationship is established. Some of the expressions that help bond the child to the Creator are:

> *Buenos días le dé Dios.* (May God grant you a good morning.)
> *Si Dios quiere.* (If God wills.)
> *Con el favor de Dios.* (With God's help, grace, goodness.)
> *Dios mediante.* (God willing.)
> *¡Bendito y alabado sea Dios!* (May God be blessed and praised!)
> *Adios.* (Good-bye. [literally, this means "I commend you to God."])
> *Así lo quiso Dios.* (It was God's will, God so "willed" it.)
> *Sea por Dios.* (Let it be according to God's will.)

God is not divorced from life. Hispanics recognize the powerful and mighty Living Presence in all its majesty and yet they address the Holy One by the familiar form of *tú* (you, thou). There is awe, great reverence and respect, even fear, but there is also profound intimacy in the divine-human relationship. One is reminded of the piety and understanding of God shared by the Spanish mystics.

The United Methodist Church has struggled to understand the uniqueness of a people that can give expression to their faith powerfully through their gifts and graces, and through their culture. In the last few years the Church has begun to accept the validity and richness of the Hispanic culture as a bona fide, genuine, authentic, basic form of Christian expression that can enrich the life of the whole church.

The adopting and adapting of certain Hispanic celebrations such as *la quinceañera* (a ceremony for fifteen-year-old girls) and *las posadas* is a sign of a committed effort to celebrate "God with us" as the family of God.

The United Methodist Church has always been a connectional church. Missionaries who went out to Latin America took with them the customs, traditions, and worship styles of the sending church. The younger churches, excited by the "good news," followed the worship patterns introduced and established by the missionaries. Their cultural traditions were dismissed because they were considered stumbling blocks for spiritual growth and thus deemed unacceptable to God. And so the separation of faith and life, religion and culture began.

Hispanics were attracted to the Methodist Church through the inspiring hymns, the dynamic preaching, the moving prayers, the powerful witnessing, and meaningful worship.

Hymns were translated from English into Spanish as were the orders of worship. Anything resembling Roman Catholic practices, such as Ash Wednesday services, candles, acolytes, *quinceañeras,* and *posadas,* was discarded and labeled non-Christian. Today, many Hispanic United Methodist churches in the United States are slowly incorporating these very elements into their worship experiences.

In 1875 the Methodist Church of Mexico published a *Book of Worship* in Spanish that included a calendar of programs for the Sunday services, scripture readings for the year, and a collection of hymns for congregational singing. The established general order of worship was to be followed, although it could be shortened at the discretion of the pastor if the circumstances so demanded it.[1] The recommendation that the General Rules be read each first Sunday of each year was still being practiced in the '50s and '60s in the church in Mexico City of which I was a member.

John and Charles Wesley, priests of the Church of England, used certain Anglican rituals within the emerging Methodist movement, but the congregations participated more in worship and they had greater freedom with regard to the order of worship, although anything that was not in accord with established religious Anglican practices was considered irregular by Wesley.

Methodists were known for their enthusiasm and fervor. Some were even called "Shouting Methodists." One of the characteristics of Hispanic Methodist worship is the religious fervor that is manifested by believers. They sing with overflowing joy and seem never to tire even after a long period of singing or even if hymns have five or more stanzas. Enthusiasm seems to be the natural climate in worship, especially in the more charismatic congregations where more *estribillos* (choruses) rather than hymns are sung. People are often moved to clap as they sing, raise their arms in praise, and play tambourines. Such lively participation is spontaneous, unavoidable, and contagious. It indeed becomes a celebration.

Hispanics have different types of worship services. There are the praise and prayer services in which the congregation feels moved to sing wholeheartedly, recite favorite Bible verses, share blessings received during the week, meditate, and pray. Testimony services are those in which participants stand up one at a time voluntarily and publicly testify in word and song about their Christian experience and their faith journey. Agape services or love feasts occur in which Christians gather to sing, fellowship, and share a meal or simple refreshments, such as bread and water.

Growing up in a Methodist church in a Spanish-speaking community in Dallas, Texas, I remember that on the first Sunday of the month the pastor would invite four boys and girls to help him (there were no women pastors then) with the serving of bread and water. The children wore short white robes similar to those worn by acolytes, and they would walk down the middle of the aisle, two on each side. In each pair, one carried the small pieces of bread and one the glasses of water. They walked slowly down the aisle, pew by pew, offering to all the gifts of bread and water. I do not remember, but I am sure the pastor must have explained the symbolism of the agape meal before it was served. This happened during the morning worship service. In the evening, bread and wine (grape juice) were used for the celebration of Holy Communion. The bread and the water were served in the pews; the bread and the wine were served at the altar rail. It has been many years since I have seen the celebration of the agape meal in any Hispanic United Methodist church.

Holy Communion is one of two sacraments observed faithfully by Hispanic United Methodists, usually on the first Sunday of the month. Dr. Roberto L. Gómez, in an article in *Apuntes,* compares Holy Communion in the Roman Catholic and in the Protestant traditions. He indicates that for the Roman Catholic, the Mass is the "center of religious life." Those who belong to that branch of Christianity participate in the Mass at least once a week and some do so on a daily basis. He goes on to say that because of the way we were evangelized and became Protestants, "the Sacrament of Holy Communion is de-emphasized." He continues that the preaching from scripture and the spontaneity of worship became more important than Holy Communion to Protestants, but that "the de-emphasis on Holy Communion is a high price to pay to become a Protestant."[2]

Hispanic United Methodist churches observe the ritual for communion found in the *Himnario Metodista* or similar rituals in Spanish, printed in worship resources published by the General Board of Discipleship. These are translations from the rituals in English. Because there is flexibility within The United Methodist Church, Hispanics are beginning to develop their own liturgy for Holy Communion as well as for other celebrations. They have discovered that they need not depend always on translated resources or they will lose the opportunity to gift the church with their faith experience and will rob the church from seeing with new eyes.

Tortillas have been used in some of the majority churches and by the organizers of events beyond the local church, as communion bread, but I have not yet seen tortillas used in Hispanic churches. Have we as Hispanics been carefully taught that only bread can be used for communion?

The United Methodist Church practices open communion, that is, anyone, church member or not, who comes to the Lord's table is offered the sacrament of bread and wine.

We are awed by the sense of mystery and the plenitude of Holy Communion. We remember how deeply God loved us in Jesus Christ, and we celebrate the opportunity to experience the living presence of Christ that we may be and live and taste the goodness of God's grace now.

Hispanics generally go as a family to the altar. Even when the congregation numbers more than a hundred, Hispanics prefer going to the altar rail rather than just walking by, taking the elements, and going back to their pews without ever kneeling and praying.

More and more churches are beginning to use the common cup and the intinction method rather than the small glasses. An offering for the poor and the needy is often left at the rail.

The other sacrament, baptism, takes on special meaning for Hispanics, for it becomes more than a family affair or a customary religious practice.

Roberto L. Gómez also talks about baptism in his article "Mestizo Spirituality." He quotes from Father Virgilio Elizondo's book *Christianity and Culture* in regard to baptism in the Hispanic context:

> One of these moments which is most important in a Latin American family is Baptism, for the people value the family highly. Baptism is the sign through which the person becomes incorporated into the

Christian community. The Spanish speaking have a profound sense of compadrazgo, the spiritual relationship that is established between the godparents and the parents of the baptized child. This bond is deeper than blood relationships because it is freely chosen and freely accepted.[3]

The majority of Hispanic parents baptize their children as infants. Each child is regarded as a gift from God not only to the parents but also to the community. Through baptism the church is declaring that the child is not an orphan and never will be because each baptized child will always be a part of the family of God.

Baptism enables the congregation to become the welcoming committee that brings the child into the faith community. Godparents are not chosen at random or haphazardly, but very carefully. The chosen godparents become part of the extended family. A bond of intimacy is affirmed between families. It is a sacred moment when godparents understand the responsibility they assume.

I belonged to a small Methodist church in Mexico City during my years of service there. It was a strong church spiritually and a very caring congregation. We were family. The pastor even said there were no poor people among us because whenever there was any kind of need, the brothers and sisters always responded splendidly.

We rejoiced when our intermediate youth counselor and her fiancé announced their engagement. Both of them came from good Christian families. Both were members of our church. She was a public school teacher and he was getting ready to graduate with a degree in architecture. He had to leave town for several weeks for business reasons, and she became lonely. She became pregnant by her fiancé's brother. His parents wanted him to do the "right thing," and he was willing to marry her, but she refused because she did not love him. The congregation was torn because it did not want to take sides or be a divided congregation. Both families were deeply loved. The pastor was wise in helping us during this critical period. Other churches would have shut the door to both families. We decided to draw the circle wide and hold them close to our hearts. They were family. We all had been baptized into the same faith. Baptism meant belonging. Eight days after the baby was born, both families came forward to present the child to God, and when she was baptized, we all vowed we would be the godparents and assured her of God's love and ours. It was a moment of remembering our baptismal vows. In that moment we knew that baptism was and is more than a ritual, fancy clothes, water, and *mole* (a Mexican dish). Baptism for Hispanics is a bonding, a very intentional bonding of God's people with the baptized person. There indeed would be no orphan, no stigma, no guilt trip for the child or parents, for God's water sprinkled over her was pure.

Guitars, other instruments, and mariachi bands are becoming more and more a part of Hispanic worship. In early 1994, a beloved church member of one of the Hispanic United Methodist churches in Dallas died. He was the music director of a Dallas high school. He had been instrumental in building pride in his Hispanic students for their culture. The mariachi band he organized played at his funeral and interment services. Mariachi bands would not have been acceptable in worship, much less funeral services, a few years ago.

Among his many gifts and legacy this brother left behind was the formation of a children's choir in his church. One year the children sang at an annual conference banquet. At first the children had no interest in singing in anything but English, but he won them over. They sing enthusiastically, joyously, blending their voices beautifully in English and Spanish. So, bilingual children's choirs are a rich resource of blessing in some of our Hispanic churches.

Does the passing of the peace during the worship service, especially a communion service, have a new or deeper meaning for Hispanics? The question arises because from the time

Hispanics enter the church building the passing of the peace begins with the embracing, the handshakes, and the holy kiss. And people will do it again after the service with the same people. They do not wait until the appropriate time in the worship service, even though they will participate again in the ritual of friendship if the order of worship or the liturgy so prescribes it. It is a vital part of the faith experience of Hispanics.

The sharing of joys and concerns is part of the worship service. People usually stand up and share what is in their hearts. Others come forward and speak and remain standing until it is time to kneel and pray. Then the pastor invites whoever wishes to come forward and kneel before the pastoral prayer is offered. Some pastors place their hands on the head or shoulders of those who have come forward to the communion rail for prayer, as he or she prays individually for each one.

God blessed the Methodist movement from the beginning by awakening within Charles and John Wesley the desire to provide hymns for the people. In fact, it has been said that Methodism was born singing. Hymns helped to spread the doctrine and the faith throughout the British Empire. John Wesley was quick yet careful in encouraging the use of folk tunes for religious purposes. He translated and adapted some Moravian hymns for Methodists to use.

Hispanic Methodists have also produced their own hymnologists and composers such as Vicente Mendoza ("Jesús es mi Rey soberano"), Federico Pagura, Mortimer Arias, Raquel Mora Martínez, Raquel Achón, Pablo Sosa, Justo L. González, Manuel V. Flores, and many others.

For many years Hispanic United Methodists in the United States used different hymnals because there was no Methodist hymnal in Spanish. Congregations were free to choose from the available Spanish hymnals. This became problematic when visiting other Methodist churches. Church members carried their Bibles and their hymnals to church with them every time they attended services. In visiting other churches or in going to meetings outside the local church, one soon discovered the confusion when everyone had a different hymnal.[4]

It is not surprising then that a committee from the Rio Grande Conference was formed under the direction of Dr. Alfredo Náñez to determine how to publish a hymnal in Spanish so that all the Spanish-speaking Methodist churches could use the same resource in worship. The purpose was not to add another hymnal to the growing list of Spanish-language hymnals, but to try to establish an order for public worship within the denomination. More than ten different hymnals were being used in the Conference.

In 1940 more than eight hundred people in Texas, New Mexico, Arizona, Colorado, California, Cuba, and Mexico were invited to send in a list of twenty favorite hymns and where these hymns could be found. The committee received more than five hundred replies. From this list the three hundred most popular hymns were considered. On January 3, 1955, the Planning Commission of the Rio Grande Conference authorized the Conference Board of Christian Education to assume responsibility for the publication of the hymnal.[5]

A month later the commission met in El Paso, Texas, to give the hymnal its final form. The hymnal, published by the Casa Bautista in El Paso, contained 252 hymns, models for orders of worship, three orders of worship, the rituals for Holy Communion and Baptism, reception of new members, and sixty responsive readings. In 1956 the Methodist Church had a Methodist hymnal in Spanish. It was well received.

About fifteen years later an effort was made to publish a more adequate hymnal to meet the growing needs of Hispanic United Methodists. The new hymnal appeared in 1973 and contained 394 hymns and 108 worship resources.[6] The rituals for Holy Communion and Baptism were included. A communion service with musical responses was also included. This second hymnal was published by The United Methodist Publishing House in Nashville. The response was overwhelming. This hymnal has now gone through several printings.

In 1992 the General Conference of The United Methodist Church authorized the publication of another hymnal, which was presented to the 1996 General Conference. Hispanic United Methodists have eagerly awaited the publication of this hymnal, edited by Raquel Mora Martínez. The theology and language of each hymn have been thoroughly studied. New worship resources are included as well as some musical settings to the psalter.

Because of the rising interest in *estribillos* (choruses), two books have already been published. Dr. Roberto Escamilla was the editor of *Celebremos* (1979)[7] and *Celebremos II* (1983). The *Celebremos II* Task Force responded to MARCHA's (Methodist Associates Representing the Cause of Hispanic Americans) recommendation that more indigenous music be used in Hispanic worship. The *estribillos* and other songs chosen had to meet the following criteria:

1. a good theological basis
2. good poetic and musical qualities
3. inclusive language
4. an awareness of spiritual and secular values
5. wholeness of thought.[8]

The compositions are presented in both English and Spanish so that non-Spanish-speaking congregations may be enriched by the message and rhythm. This effort was also intended to help the church at large to understand the contributions that Hispanic United Methodists can make to their worship experience. This second book contains forty-six songs and most now bear names of poets and composers. These books, too, were well received.

Spontaneous prayer continues to be a vital part of Hispanic worship. Written prayers are used, but the pastor or liturgist often calls upon a church member to lead the congregation in prayer. I have not yet heard anyone say, "No, I can't."

In many churches the congregation stands when any portion of scripture is read, not just the Gospels. Hispanics accept both Testaments as the inspired Word of God. Many people, especially adults, still carry their Bibles with them to church even when there are Bibles in the pews.

A special celebration in a worship context is "la quinceañera," the time when a young girl celebrates her fifteenth birthday. It is a way of presenting her to the community and declaring that she is now ready for responsibility. Earlier in the century it was a way for parents to present their daughter to society and say, "She is available for marriage and motherhood." There is no such celebration for a male youth. The quinceañera dresses in white and is escorted toward the altar by a young man, generally of her own choosing. They are followed by fifteen young men and fifteen young women who accompany them in this special occasion. The worship service includes congregational singing, prayers, scripture readings, music, a sermon, and an allusive liturgy. Padrinos and madrinas ("sponsors") present the quinceañera with special gifts, such as a Bible, jewelry, and coins. The community joins the parents in thanking God for their daughter and praying that God may grant her life, joy, and health. After the worship service, there is a party or reception.

Most Hispanic United Methodist churches have not followed the pattern of the majority church in canceling the Sunday evening services and midweek Bible studies. These services are generally more informal. There is more singing; people usually choose their favorite hymns, and explain why they like them. Singing may go on for thirty to sixty minutes. Also, this is the time when many congregations sing *estribillos* or learn new hymns. It is also a time for quoting favorite Bible verses, offering prayers, listening to God's Word, and from time to time dialoguing with the pastor on a scripture passage.

A book of the Bible is usually chosen for careful examination and reflection during the midweek Bible study. There are also prayers and hymn singing.

A service that is becoming more and more a part of Hispanic United Methodist worship is the one observed on Ash Wednesday. Until recently it had not been part of Hispanic Methodist tradition. It still is not a part of Methodist tradition in most Latin American churches. Because it was a Roman Catholic religious practice, it did not become a part of the liturgy of the Hispanic United Methodist churches at first.

Most Hispanic United Methodists observe Ash Wednesday as the beginning of the Lenten season. It serves to remind Hispanics of their mortality and calls them to reflect on their relationship to God and to their neighbors. The ashes are either bought or made from the palms used on Palm Sunday the year before. They are blessed and placed on the foreheads of the faithful during a worship service. A cross is traced with the ashes as words are pronounced by the pastor, who also invites the congregation to enter into a season of prayer, reflection, Bible study, and good works, and to choose a spiritual discipline during Lent. To receive ashes implies one is willing to humble oneself before God, that one is willing to participate in the suffering of Jesus. Most Hispanic United Methodists do not make vows to fast or abstain from eating certain foods or from participating in certain activities. Submitting to a disciplined life during this period is difficult for many. Some churches offer Lenten studies dividing the congregation into cluster groups, each with a lay leader.

Hispanic United Methodists generally have the same worship services and activities that other churches do during Holy Week: Holy Communion and/or foot washing service on Maundy Thursday; a service on the seven last words, or a dramatic presentation and the stripping of the sanctuary on Good Friday; and a sunrise service on Easter Sunday. A breakfast usually follows the early morning or sunrise Easter service. Special music by church choirs highlights the resurrection message at the regular worship service on Easter morning.

Another special celebration for Methodists comes on May twenty-fourth when some congregations bring to mind John Wesley's conversion experience, when he felt his heart strangely warmed. It is a time to sing Wesleyan hymns and remember how God can help us see that the world is our parish, too.

Hispanic United Methodists have been researching the tradition of *las posadas,* because it has not been a part of our religious experience. It is an attempt to reenact Mary's and Joseph's search for an inn in Bethlehem. Children learn about this tradition in school, but there has been little written to help The United Methodist Church celebrate this tradition.

When I arrived in Mexico the Methodist Church of Mexico was having *noches invernales* (winter nights) during the nine nights the secular world was having *posadas* (that is, parties with much drinking). What The Methodist Church of Mexico did was to provide religious services and a celebration for nine consecutive nights. Each church organization was assigned one night. Each organization was responsible for the worship service, the refreshments, the piñatas, and the fruit and candy bags, and each group was encouraged to be as creative as possible. Some organizations, especially the youth, presented dramas or pageants, some rather spectacular. It was a time for worship and fellowship. These activities were always well attended.

Worship services are not restricted to one hour. It is not that time is not important to Hispanics, but rather that when the Spirit of God is given control of the worship experience, God cannot be bound by time and space. Hispanics stay around until they have greeted all their friends after the service, even though many greeted one another before the service. There is no rush to beat the Baptists to the cafeteria line.

More Hispanic pastors are becoming lectionary preachers. For many Hispanics, the sermon is the heart of the worship service. Congregations expect powerful and inspiring messages. The preacher is free to be genuinely expressive. There need not be a revival or an evangelistic service for the preacher to have an altar call. In many congregations it is essential that the pastor be bilingual, for both preaching and ministry. A bilingual liturgy is used in such churches.

The captors of the Hebrew exiles in Babylonia taunted them by saying, "Sing us a song from your country" (Ps. 137:3 author's translation). And the exiles cried out, "How can we sing if we are so far from our homes and our land?" The large number of immigrants from Latin America in the United States could easily raise the same question, "How can we sing in a foreign land when all we hear is 'Speak English only'?" The saying *Tan lejos de Dios y tan cerca de los Estados Unidos* (So far from God and so close to the United States) becomes a living nightmare.

The Hispanic United Methodist churches are here to say to the stranger and alien that God is here and that there are resources in their own language that can assure them they are *en su casa con la familia de Dios* (at home with the family of God). Thus they can sing and worship in a foreign land where there is freedom to do so in one's own language.

A saying in Spanish goes *muchos amenes al cielo llegan* (literally "many amens get up to heaven" or, "the one who perseveres goes far"). As Hispanics we have persevered and will continue to do so because of our desire to worship in spirit and in truth in our own tongue and tradition, experiencing the oneness of faith and life, religion and culture.

# CHAPTER FIVE

Miguel Angel Darino

# What Is Different About Hispanic Baptist Worship?

The purpose of this work is to present a brief study of worship forms among Baptists. We shall focus this study in the North American context while considering some biblical, historical, and cultural aspects relevant to Hispanic worship practice. Although I am a member of the American Baptist Church (U.S.A.), references will not be limited to these churches, but to what is happening in Hispanic Baptist churches in general.

It is undeniable that among Hispanic Baptists, worship maintains the same traditional characteristics currently as it has throughout Baptist history: constant evolution, study, discussion, and criticism. The belief and practice of congregational autonomy and interdependence has opened the way for His-

panic Baptist worship to stand out through a wide gamut of
styles and forms. These forms span traditional to contemporary; from early heritage to currently emerging trends; from
the purely Anglo to the mostly Hispanic; and from orthodox
liturgy to free forms of expression. The latter is indicative of
existing elements, as much cultural as theological, which
should be taken into account in order to form a more realistic
analysis of worship among Hispanic Baptists. The variety of
styles and forms is not exclusive of Hispanics, even less so of
Hispanic Baptists; nevertheless, in this ethnic context such
variety is more noticeable, probably due to the influence of
certain movements nearer to us in history, both in Latin
America and in the United States. In a very special way the
charismatic and neopentecostal movements have made a significant impact on the life and development of Hispanic
churches.[1] The impact of these movements on church life has
led Hispanic Baptists to a recognition of the need for evaluation and reconsideration of their own forms of expression in
the practice of worship. In many cases this is discussed on the
basis of cultural reality rather than from theological founda-
tions—which nevertheless should not be taken as deliberately
ignoring biblical and theological issues. What it definitely
shows is a deep yearning and search for a better defined cultural
expression of worship.

It is precisely in this cultural aspect that a great difference
should be taken into account between what is done in the
American context and what is done elsewhere. The heteroge-
neity existing in the United States unfailingly affects the
expression of worship. The subject at hand, as I personally
understand it, has more to do with the form of worship of
Hispanic Baptists in this environment marked by various
influences on heritage, culture, and social context, than necessarily with the traditional culture.

It has been said: "Culture is an irritating subject." Yet it may
not be separated from history or from other cultures, since no

culture exists without another.[2] We must not ignore the historical reality of being influenced by a variety of cultures. Hispanics, having their own social, cultural, and political features, are influenced when inserted in a different social environment. The outcome is a new and even more complex expression of worship. That is why, to reach a clearer comprehension of Hispanic Baptists' devotion and thought, it is necessary to understand the development of their spiritual life.

For Baptists, Christian worship is an encounter with God—that is, a dialogue, revelation, and answer. God reveals Godself to human beings and the human being responds to that revelation.[3] This revelation may come through Bible reading, preaching, hymns, baptism, or communion, and among Baptists it is understood to be received and reasserted in corporate worship. A Baptist believes that the evolution of spiritual life finds its strongest foundation in the doctrinal conception of the priesthood of every believer, which shapes itself into sense and practice within the parameters of the local congregation. So it is important and significant to mention the constant struggle of Baptists since their early beginnings, to stand by the Bible as the center of authority and faith, as much in reference to doctrines as in the practice of congregational worship.

Although it is true that some efforts have been made of late in the area of congregational worship,[4] it is impossible to speak of a Baptist theology of worship. Not that there is not one, but rather that there has never been to this day, a comprehensive liturgy that is common to all Baptists—or one common to all Hispanic Baptists.

It could be said that even before its formal beginnings, in the middle of the seventeenth century, Baptist worship was known for its firm adherence to the roots, and a brave spirit of reaction against liturgic systems established and guaranteed by the state. An example was the protests against the Anglican Church.[5] The Anabaptists made their appearance in England, while fleeing from cruel persecution all over Europe. This persecution was enthusiastically sponsored by Catholics as well as by classical reformers such as Luther, Zwingli, and Calvin.[6] There was no place where Anabaptists could find peace and freedom. Even in England they were persecuted and burned at the stake. There were also radical groups who had to flee to Amsterdam when persecution overtook them. These separatists, while living in Holland, would meet with Anabaptists and Mennonites. Nevertheless, the reaction against established systems was not born of mere caprice: it was a natural occurrence, the outcome of a conviction, a particular understanding of the Holy Scriptures.

Through the years, the main concern of Baptists has been to keep the purity of their doctrinal beliefs in relation to their understanding of truth in the Bible. For that reason it is not strange that all theology called "Baptist" starts with a deep consideration of the Holy Scriptures. The same must be said about their theology of worship.[7]

In spite of the fact that there are few historical documents that clearly illustrate Baptist tradition of private and public worship, it is nevertheless possible to distinguish some groups of separatists and radicals that had great influence on the Baptists. This will help toward a partial understanding of the nature of Baptist worship. Within these groups the Anabaptists, the Reformed Churches, the Puritans, and Free Churches are found. The Baptists received especially strong influence from the Anabaptists. The latter were formed by a radical group arisen in 1527 in Grossmunster, Switzerland, known originally as "The Swiss Brethren."[8] They based their movement on baptism of believers and the rejection of infant baptism. They engaged the doctrinal conviction of the absolute need of personal commitment with Jesus Christ, most surely influenced by the worship practice of the free and independent churches.

The first congregation that could be called Baptist came into being through John Smyth in 1609.[9] It was formed by a group of believers who met illegally in England and later immigrated to Amsterdam. They acquired and practiced some of the basic doctrines of the Anabaptists—for example, baptism of believers, and other liturgical elements previously mentioned, such as Bible readings, prayers, and so forth, which later formed the foundation of their worship expression. Ernest Alexander Payne, General Secretary to the Baptist Union of Great Britain and Ireland, makes mention of an interesting letter sent by Hugh and Anne Bromehead, a couple belonging to the congregation of John Smyth in Amsterdam, to a relative of theirs in England. The letter dates back to the year 1609 and gives a description of public worship in that church:

> The order of the worship and government of our church is: I. We begin with a prayer, after read some one or two chapters of the Bible; give the sense thereof and confer upon the same; that done, we lay aside our books and after a solemn prayer made by the first speaker he propoundeth some text out of the scripture and prophesieth out of the same by the space of one hour to three quarters of an hour. After him standeth up a second speaker and prophesieth out of the said text the like time and space, sometimes more, sometimes less. After him, the third, the fourth, the fifth &c., as the time will give leave. Then the first speaker concludeth with prayer as he began with prayer, with an exhortation to contribution to the poor, which collection being made is also concluded with prayer. This morning exercise begins at eight of the clock and continueth unto twelve of the clock. The like course of exercise is observed in the afternoon from two of the clock unto five or six of the clock. Last of all the execution of the government of the Church is handled.[10]

This is one of the first known descriptions of a Baptist service, revealing how the Bible was central to, and the inspiration for, worship. Congregational worship included many hours of Bible reading, the participation of laity, exhortation, preaching, and later, congregational singing and the Lord's Supper.[11] The Lord's Supper became a fundamental element in Baptist worship primarily because of three elements: the background of the Reformation, the special influence of the Mennonites, and the dynamic vitality that Benjamin Keach introduced into the church. It was revitalized by a deeper sense of worship of our Lord Jesus Christ in contrast to "means of grace," as it had been before the Reformation. It was celebrated once a month, usually at a special evening service.[12] We may well say at this point that the Mennonites did not agree with the Baptist practice of allowing laity to minister the ordinances in the absence of a pastor or minister.[13]

Comparing this information to the reality of Baptist worship services today, we find certain interesting facts. On the one hand we recognize that the centrality of the Bible is the traditional foundation of public worship among Baptists, a nonnegotiable principle. While on the other hand, the order of worship service described above should also be taken into account as a historical basis from which the classic "Baptist worship service" developed, and is still practiced in many Baptist circles presently. The difference is not that great when we take a global perspective. Were we to describe a typical Baptist service of today we would eliminate very few elements from our description and would add only a minimum. This can be clearly detected when we observe basic types of Baptist worship from 1695 to 1994, as presented by G. Thomas Halbrooks[14] and also Ken Hemphill and Larry White.[15]

However, just as there is no common manual or book of worship for Baptists, there is neither a model of worship nor a common theology of worship. Baptists consider the maintenance of public worship, based on scriptural patterns of carefully studied worship, to be a vital part of church life. For this reason many Baptist leaders through the years have assumed that the importance of worship is not centered in the discussion over location, symbols, or the different forms of liturgic expressions. Its importance lies in the fact that the church is not a building, but people. So worship is an encounter with

God, all together in the sanctuary, all of us responding together to the Divine Presence, with a profound sense of power and grace within. This is where the Baptist doctrinal conception of congregationalism and universal priesthood of believers is manifested. This is important because it marks the Baptist idea of worship. The Baptist worship service is a congregational service where "everyone" participates. Although it is important to point out that the conception of congregationalism and priesthood should not be considered exclusive of the Baptists, the fact still remains that these have always been part of Baptist identity. In other words they are distinctive principles traditionally defended by the Baptists through the years.

Before entering into the consideration of our modern reality on the subject of Hispanic Baptist worship, I must mention another Baptist element that I consider part of our tradition that we have "lost along the way." I am referring to the charismatic element. Unfortunately, when charismatic worship is mentioned we usually think of the Pentecostal charismatic pattern, or the other movements to which I have already referred at the beginning of this work. Nevertheless, before the historic birth of Pentecostalism, worship among Baptists was distinguished by its spontaneity and, as I have said, by its participation. James Barry refers to this as follows:

> Jesus said, "If the Son sets you free, you will be free indeed" (John 8:36). Baptists have taken this promise seriously. They always have claimed the total right of following the leadership of the Holy Spirit in planning for and conducting worship services.[16]

When the first Baptist church in the present-day United States was founded under the direction of Roger Williams (1639), the founders also implanted the European style of worship.[17] As we know, this style consisted of long hours of reading, but it also included spontaneous expressions in the power of the Holy Spirit, especially for leaders and preachers who began to prophesy after receiving a message from God.

This form of Baptist worship had its effervescence (later known as "The Period of the Frontier Revival") as Justo Anderson states, when "as a result of an extraordinary visitation of the Holy Spirit, England and the United States were shaken from their spiritual lethargy."[18]

It is significant that the Baptists were born as a denomination in the middle of the seventeenth century, before the process of urbanization and professionalization in the United States frontier. It is in the "fire of revival" that Baptists took denominational form. This revival had its origin in the Anglican Church, characterized by powerful preaching with the purpose of giving conviction of sin, preaching of laity, strong emotional experiences, congregational singing, and so forth.[19]

Although some researchers do not openly recognize and scarcely mention this fact, the standards of this revival became part of the Evangelical Baptist identity. The Baptist way of preaching (which is revivalist), the invitation to approach the altar, the kneeling, and the call were acquired during the appearance of the denomination emerging in the midst of revival. We must recognize that Baptists resisted this movement at the beginning. Nevertheless when the fire of the revival came to an end among the Congregationalists, with some Presbyterians and Methodists, it was the Baptists who received the greater benefit from this "golden age." This explains why Baptists are the largest Protestant denomination in the United States.

The dramatic reality we are currently facing is that for some reason this spiritual fervor characteristic of the Baptists lingered and remained in the past as historical information, as genetics, in the background. The forms are still present, but not the experience. In other words, the forms of worship have been maintained but the substance is missing. It could be said that the forms that became traditionally institutionalized advanced over the spiritual experience. I use the word *traditionally* because the very Baptist idiosyncrasy does not permit a decreed or formal institutionalization. An example of this can be given in the type of Baptist service currently practiced, especially among Anglo-Saxons and in some Hispanic Baptist circles, where traditional hymns are sung almost as a conditioned reflex, but they do not produce the spiritual impact of a century ago when they were sung over and over again, a hundred times a day, in the swell of revival. That is why Baptists in the dominant Anglo-Saxon culture are seeking new patterns of worship.

From the cultural point of view in the majority of Hispanic contexts, worship was European–North American until the middle of this century. Hispanics worshiped according to established patterns. In other words, as they opened their hearts to the gospel, they also received the forms of worship. Christian organizations that emerged from last century's revival began sending missionaries to different countries. Those missionaries, motivated by the fervor of that time, took not only the gospel with them, but also patterns of worship from different sources, both European and North American. In reality these patterns were transplanted.[20] This transposition of European–North American forms of worship could be evidenced in hymnology, in the liturgy used at the time, and in the style of music and worship. In other words, as the gospel reached Hispanics via Europe and North America, established patterns were based on aspects of North Atlantic worship. What we have just described is what came to us: a style of worship descended from the nineteenth-century revival and gospel hymns.

Following an awakening among Hispanics in the '60s, a search for a more genuine and authentic form of worship began. This was a time in which a general desire was felt to worship God from the depths of one's being, just as one is, not from a "second nature," which is called by some a "subculture."[21] This is where the autochthonous element enters; the wish to assume responsibility in various ways is manifested as much in the direction of the life and work of the church, in general, as in the idea of a real Hispanic theology. Hispanics began to think that theology should not be the patrimony of Germany or North America and should not necessarily have to come from those countries. In short, there was a general feeling among Hispanics that they also might be entitled to a form of theology that was authentically their own.

In the area of worship, this feeling of entitlement means that the forms then being used were culturally alien. Styles of worship had to be reconsidered. A great variety of styles appeared as this feeling grew stronger. Hispanics should not necessarily follow European and North American forms. The latter are rooted in specific cultural soils. It should be the same in the case of Hispanics. It was then that there was an opening to and consciousness of the fact that forms of worship may need a change, or evolution, if they were really to reflect our lives and concerns. So Hispanics, wishing to pursue this line of biblical understanding, began to elaborate, rethink, and produce change. The phenomenon began in Latin America and new opportunity arose when these ideas reached the United States. The United States was open to change, possibly because of the social revolution of the '60s.[22]

Hispanics were longing for a return to their roots. From a cultural point of view there are certain elements in worship such as music, for example, that the worshiper needs to own in order for the act of praise to be truly significant. For the Hispanic, a return to roots comes, perhaps, with the use of a guitar in the place of an organ or a piano. At the same time, drums are introduced, reflecting a combination of influences that have shaped our culture: African, Central and South American, and even North American, for many of the drums used were set up in drum batteries as is common in North American popular music.

Because of immigration, Hispanic Baptist churches in the U.S.A. have acquired special characteristics. Two of the most common are: (1) the representation of various nationalities; in some cases as many as fifteen countries are represented in a congregation of one hundred people; and (2) the presence of several denominational backgrounds in the same congregation.

This reality creates a conflict in the area of formal worship. For example, the Hispanic who arrives in the United States, having known the gospel of salvation in her native country, brings with her a scheme or a model that she has absorbed, which has been "filtered" and influenced by at least three different cultures. The style of worship brought in by this Hispanic has already existed here before: It came from Europe and the United States through the work of missionaries, and is now returning to the United States by way of an alien culture.

Now if that style of worship, which has been practiced for years, has driven Hispanic Baptists to the point of having to evaluate and reconsider their forms of cultic or worship expression, then a greater crisis exists. If an Anglo with his tradition, genetic information, and background is not spiritually moved by a hymn, then to a Hispanic it says even less. In past generations the religious and cultural background available to a Hispanic, believer or unbeliever, acquired consciously or unconsciously was Roman Catholicism. This is not the background of an Anglo-Saxon. That is to say that the average Hispanic Baptist knows little of what the Great Awakening was, or of the Second Great Awakening, and even less of the enormous expansion on the frontier that became the main source of Baptist growth. Nevertheless, due to a kind of cultural imitation, from a desire to "be Anglo" and to be accepted, a Hispanic will face this culture, pick up a hymnbook, and sing hymns that neither mean nor represent anything to him or her. So here we find the Hispanic Baptist, singing a hymn in church and listening to his or her "real music" at home. It is the latter that finds an echo in the soul.

The question is: Why does he not take *Polo Negrete* to church? Why does she not take *música caliente* to church? Why does she not take salsa, mambo, ranchera, or tango to church? Simply because he is afraid. Because there is a dichotomy in her. She has been taught that "Anglo" tradition is sacred and the other is profane. We do not mean to ignore the precious heritage of classical hymnology that we consider part of our evangelical culture, yet unfortunately many hymns are the personal experiences of Christians in other times and other contexts and are out of place in our times, especially for Hispanics.[23]

This situation becomes more complex in certain cases due to a loss of identity, or rather to an identity conflict. This has proved to be the fact in Baptist congregations formed by people of Hispanic origin who do not master the Spanish language and do not have a deep knowledge of their roots; often they are first- or second-generation Hispanics. This group is immersed in churches where the style of worship is a carbon copy of Anglo patterns. One can perceive something "Hispanic" even if only from their brown skins, or their "tamales, burritos, and frijoles" on the tables in the Saturday evening social gatherings.

If we compare this reality with the experience of most Anglo-Saxons in worship (an institutionalization of the form and a loss of the contents) we shall discover a highly significant fact.[24] The Hispanic has a different appreciation of the gospel. She suffers a shock in a church that has merged into the surrounding culture. The Hispanic Baptist has a clear concept that to be an evangelical is to live one's evangelism and that not doing so is not being Christian.

The Hispanic Christian knows well that there is a dividing line between Christian and unbeliever, which means that, once crossed, one is in the world—in an alien land. In the present North American setting, the Hispanic believer finds a church that is fused with society and culture. At the beginning, the church spread within the culture and impacted it; however, currently the dividing line has become vague and diffused. No longer is there a clearly defined demarcation: People come and go from the church to the world and back again. This reality has been a factor that has diluted the contents of the gospel in its various forms. Of course among Anglo-Saxons the concept of "the world" is unknown. But whether "here" or "there" we as Hispanics have clichés: "the world," "he went back to the world," "the influence of the world."

Furthermore, the church has caused people to be "spectators" of what is called worship, performed by a few people behind a pulpit. This has produced a vacuum in the Anglo-Saxon culture that causes worshipers to feel a need for new patterns that can return the freshness to the church. When Anglos watch Hispanics worship they feel there is something in these people that brings great joy to their church life. And so there is. But that life is not superficial; it is not in certain transient forms, for such forms may be accidental. The excitement and impulse of the Hispanic church was present even before we began exploring new forms of worship. It comes precisely from shaping our lifestyle after the gospel, from seriously taking into account that boundary between church and world.

What happens in the Baptist context is that many Anglo churches see in the Hispanics their last hope. In many instances churches are dying, are on the point of closing down, and are longing for that Hispanic "vitality." Yet it would be very sad indeed if, as Hispanics did of Anglo worship, they were simply to copy the various forms of Hispanic worship, without having access to that rich original experience that brings real power into church life. This is, in other words, what we wish to convey: We hope that the Anglo-Saxon will not misinterpret— and therefore miss—the real issue at hand. It is not a matter of drums, noise, and "ballyhoo." All of that is only on the surface.

Actually, there is something else behind this exterior: comprehension, understanding of what the gospel really is, and all
that we hope the Hispanic—even while living in this society—
may never lose. For we have maintained it for a long time and
that has awakened the spirit of the church. As far as I can
understand this is a vital affair, the pivotal point. It has to do
with spirituality. It has to do with the doctrinal points of
conversion, holiness, justification, and other factors that have
been a concern for the Baptists through their history—although I cannot deal with these subjects here.

Unfortunately, in many cases among Hispanic Baptists in
the United States, a renewal of worship is thought to be only
a change of form. For some, renewal means simply to change
the classical order of service, to retire the hymnbook, and to
establish a pattern that in the long run may turn out the same
formal vacuum against which the church is trying to fight.
Even when we speak of adding a Hispanic flavor to preaching,
or when we refer to "Hispanic theology," quite often we are
still immersed in a liturgy that, in spite of all the new forms,
is not culturally distinctive, one that is not ours because it does
not reflect our profound understanding of the gospel.

That is why Hispanic Baptists do not have a common
worship pattern. We are going through a time of transition and
conflict, faced with the reality of having to maintain the vitality
that the church has shown along the years, and with the added
burden of being inserted in a totally different social context.
The vitality of the Hispanic church does not center on a style
of worship, but on an understanding of the gospel. It starts
from having a serious view of God's Kingdom and a life
according to the Will of God, never blending or mixing church
with society, culture, or the world in general.

In a way, this is just being felt by the Anglo-Saxons as they
watch our worship. Their religious life is being permeated by
the manifested need of many to become not only spectators,
but protagonists in the worship experience. Although there

will always be Hispanics who will wish to cover up this reality, it is something latent and felt at least among the Baptists at present. This problem may not be considered important by other denominations, but it is of vital importance among Baptists. It is based upon the historic principle that declares: "The Church is a congregation of regenerated people."[25] It is not baptism but regeneration that makes a Christian.

Nevertheless, in these days of transition and conflict that the Baptists are experiencing, not all is negative regarding this worship or cultic practice. As previously mentioned, from the beginning, the belief in the autonomy of the local church among Baptists allows for freedom of choice in the style and emphasis of worship. In this sense each Baptist church follows a liturgy or cultural practice whether good or bad, formal or spontaneously free, traditional or contemporary, but has not, up to now, lost the basic and historic elements necessary for a Christian worship service.

J. C. Ryle mentions seven elements that should be included to distinguish a Christian worship service: (1) honoring the Lord's Day; (2) the ministers should guide the people; (3) the preaching of the Word; (4) public prayer; (5) public reading of the scriptures; (6) public praise; (7) observance of the ordinances of baptism and the Lord's Supper.[26]

It is undeniable that the greatest tension in Baptist worship today is found between what are called "traditional" and "contemporary" worship. When we explore the values of each form, we discover great treasures able to perform changes in the life of the worshiper and of the church. Many traditionalists wish for things to continue as they are. This means that they choose to follow the same course for the short time of life before them.[27]

Those who stand for the contemporary style of worship are weary of the sameness and are eager for free, less rigid forms. It is to be expected that this time of transition and search will reach two goals: (1) a balance of styles and forms of worship, beneficial to all, and (2) a discovery that the richness of worship does not consist of adding to or taking away from a certain liturgy, nor does it consist of superficial imitations already mentioned. The evidence of the Presence of God and the Holy Spirit in worship lies in a transformation of the human being made manifest in cultic practice, service, and Christian commitment, which becomes a reality after the act of worship.

In the majority of Hispanic Baptist churches there is a growing fervor in the expression of worship. Beyond the question of forms and styles, we trust that this enthusiasm will be a result of Christian living. May it be an honest response to God who has made a spiritual impact on our lives; may it be worship that flows, that creates; may there be a hymnology that emerges with the characteristic features of a culture that I represent. May there be a service where song and liturgy are no longer an imitation of something that was good, wonderful, and extraordinary in its time, but something that rises from the inner being, here and now. Let worship be what it was in the past, with the addition of present freshness—without ignoring tradition, which enriches and helps us on our way to a clear concept of what God has done during the years. If tradition is ignored, there is a danger in a loss of roots; and a tree without roots will not stand.

We seek to have a living experience of worship without ignoring the present changes, conflicts, and realities; to live an experience of worship, be it traditional or contemporary. What is important is that we reflect a clear and faithful image before the world—not a pattern or a style, but a clear and living relation with the God whom we adore and humankind needs.

# CHAPTER Six

Teresa Chávez Sauceda

# Becoming a Mestizo Church

The first time my husband and I attended worship at Iglesia Presbiteriana Getsemaní it was Mother's Day. During the worship service, the children all came forward for a presentation of songs and poems. At the conclusion, the children gave a rose to each mother in the congregation. Although my own two daughters were not yet born, I graciously accepted the rose offered to me by a timid child, not wanting to embarrass him. I was thankful for this child, whose hesitation indicated he was not sure what to do, but whose actions indicated a preference to err on the side of inclusion rather than exclusion.

With a simple gesture this child welcomed us into the family of Gethsemane Presbyterian Church. My husband and I had attended several churches since moving to Ft. Worth. This was the one we would join. Here we both found something we recognized, something that made us feel at home despite the differences in our own religious backgrounds.

I was raised in a suburban, middle-class, Anglo, Presbyterian church. My father is Hispanic, from northern New Mexico, and a graduate of Menaul, a Presbyterian high school in Albuquerque. My mother is Anglo, from the Midwest, with deep Puritan roots. My contact with Hispanic churches up to that time consisted mainly of occasional visits to the Spanish-speaking congregation in San Francisco, where my parents had many friends. My husband grew up Catholic in a south Texas barrio where English was a second language, and being Mexican was synonymous with being Catholic.

At Gethsemane the language was Spanish and the order of worship was distinctively Presbyterian, but our sense of connection went beyond finding a familiar language and ritual. Our experience reflects the complex relationship between culture and worship. I use the term *culture* here in its broadest sense—as the worldview of a people, the norms and patterns of life of a community, their spoken and symbolic language.

The act of worship cannot be separated from culture. Culture is the vehicle through which we express our faith in God, the tools we use to give praise to God, the words and images by which we pray to God. Similarly, the structure and content of worship, the language used, and the values expressed create a cultural context of their own apart from the social environment in which we live. The significance of this relationship between culture and worship has often gone unrecognized and unexamined in the church.

This bridge between culture and both faith and worship carries traffic in two directions. For the Hispanic congregation, the expression of their Christian faith is conveyed most fully as an integral part of who they are. Similarly, their understanding of what it means to be Hispanic is shaped by their experience of Christian faith.[1] As the product largely of missionary efforts, Hispanic Presbyterian churches are faithful bearers of the Reformed tradition. Some critics would even argue that they have kept the tradition too well, that they have given up too much of their own mestizo cultural heritage to become Presbyterian. If the language, music, art, and symbols one uses in worship to express one's faith are products of one's cultural identity, then one might well ask, Who are Hispanic Presbyterians?

While it is important for the church to examine its historical approach to mission and evangelism with a critical eye, the assumption that Hispanic Presbyterian congregations have lost all ties with their cultural heritage may move too quickly to label them cultural victims and overlook some of the strengths of the Hispanic congregation. The degree to which Hispanic cultural norms and mores survive, despite historical efforts to convert both culture and faith, provides the foundation for the recovery of more explicit expressions of Hispanic culture in the worship of Hispanic congregations. Their struggle to claim and sustain their identity as both Hispanic and Presbyterian bears prophetic witness to our denomination as we seek to be the church, the family of God, in a multicultural society.

As the mother of two children growing up in a very secular society, I have become very aware of the contrast between the cultural norms and values of the society in which we live and the norms and values I want to teach my children as Christians. In many respects, the chasm between these two worlds is greater than the differences between the Mexicano/Hispano/Anglo cultures of their family heritage, perhaps because these are all rooted in Christian faith.

As a parent, I depend upon the church to provide a community of faith in which to raise my children. In this context, worship is not just an hour on Sunday morning to replenish my own spiritual well; it is an important part of the education, training, and nurturing of my children's faith journey. The processes of a cultural *mestizaje* go on each Sunday, and anytime the church gathers, as the children (both young and old) of this modern technological, materialistic culture encounter the norms and values of biblical faith in a context defined by Presbyterian traditions. As Christians in a secular society we are all "bicultural" people. We stand in the same position as all mestizo peoples, able to choose what is affirming, empowering, and expressive of God's will in our lives from the traditions of our religious past and the cultural diversity that is found both in the church and in our society.

Hispanic Presbyterian congregations, by nature of who they are, have had to struggle with the questions of culture, identity, worship, and mission as a community of faith in a very intentional and self-conscious way. Gethsemane, like many Hispanic Presbyterian congregations, is a multilingual, multicultural, and multigenerational congregation. It is not uncommon on a Sunday morning for there to be three, even four generations of the same family in the pews. While the grandparents may only speak Spanish, the youngest generations may only speak English. In this context, the question of which language to use in worship becomes a critical one. Hispanic congregations have shown both courage and creativity as they have confronted this issue and explored a variety of ways of responding to the needs of the congregation.

The discussion that goes on around the issue of language and the choices that are made in Hispanic congregations reveal a great deal about values, identity, and the role of culture as the means by which we express our faith. The suggestion that at least some portion of the worship service be in English usually comes about because of the number of children and young people who are not fluent in Spanish and are thereby marginalized by a monolingual worship experience.

"The children are our future" is a cliché we often hear. What Hispanic congregations are recognizing is that if our children are to be the church of the future, they must be the church today. Their participation in the church needs to be meaningful for them both as Christians and as Hispanics in order for them to feel that it is a place where they belong. At the same time, the Hispanic church is committed to providing worship in Spanish for those older generations and recent immigrants who are most comfortable speaking in Spanish.

Thus, the conflict around language is a product of the congregation's commitment to be fully inclusive, to enable each and every member of the family to participate in worship. As the dialogue about language continues, it has raised important questions about identity and mission for Hispanic congregations. In choosing to be both a church for the Spanish speaker and a church for English-dominant Hispanics, Hispanic congregations have rejected a negative, limiting definition of themselves. Hispanic congregations see themselves as something more than a non-English-speaking Presbyterian church, more than being merely a means to an end, a way station for the culturally unassimilated.

Hispanic congregations are recognizing that what is at stake is their identity as a community of faith. They are opting to be a different kind of Presbyterian, to be *Hispanic* Presbyterians. They are opting to be a mestizo church, where Hispanic culture and Reformed tradition are both affirmed. What Hispanic congregations want to pass on to their children is both their religious tradition and their cultural identity. Thus, worshiping in Spanish is as important for the children, for whom Spanish is a second language, as it is for the grandparents, for whom Spanish is their primary language.

The discussion that has gone on in most Hispanic churches about the use of language in worship has served to bring about a clearer recognition of the degree to which Hispanic Presbyterians value their Hispanic heritage and desire to express their faith, to praise and pray to God in ways that reflect who they are as a people, rather than to adopt exclusively the forms and symbols of another people and culture.

As Hispanic congregations struggle with the issue of language, they are also recognizing that while language is a major
carrier of culture, it is not the only one. My Mother's Day story
is an example of the way in which Hispanic culture is infused
in the structures of Reformed tradition, making it a distinct
experience.

The observance of Mother's Day is certainly not unique to
Hispanic churches. Although I am increasingly suspicious each
year that Mother's Day was invented by the makers of greeting
cards, and my liturgy professor in seminary would certainly
want us to question what is the basis in scripture or liturgical
tradition for observing this essentially secular occasion, the
second Sunday in May usually gets at least a nod from the
pulpit in most North American churches. Each year, Sunday
school teachers across the country routinely plan a special craft
activity, something for the kids to give to Mom.

Dr. Roberto Gómez, who teaches in the Mexican-American
Program at Perkins School of Theology of Southern Methodist University, claims that after Christmas and Easter, the most
holy day in the life of all Mexican-American Christians, both
Protestant and Catholic, is Mother's Day. The Virgen de
Guadalupe, the "Indian representation of Mary the Mother of
Jesus," is an immensely powerful cultural and religious symbol
in Mexican culture. For the mestizo Protestant, who has
"doctrinal problems with the idea of the Virgen," Gómez
suggests the celebration of *el Día de las Madres* may be the one
remaining link, albeit an unconscious one, to the Virgen de
Guadalupe.[2]

There is another cultural factor also at work that distin-
guishes the celebration of Mother's Day in Hispanic congregations from its observance in other congregations. The
dominant culture in our society is an increasingly individual-
istic one. Despite the political rhetoric about family values,
what is really valued is individual achievement. As the oppor-
tunities have opened up for women to achieve on an individual

basis in ministry, business, education, the arts, politics, and more, there is an increasing ambivalence about Mother's Day. Apparently, the fear is that if we honor women in their role as mother, we are somehow demeaning their accomplishments in other aspects of their lives.

To the extent that family is valued in the dominant culture, it is the small nuclear family that is upheld as the norm, a norm that is increasingly in conflict with the reality of people's lives. In Hispanic culture, family is a wide, extended circle including grandparents, aunts, uncles, and cousins. This circle is extended even further to include *padrinos* or godparents, who then become *compadres* of the child's natural parents—a relationship formalized in the Catholic tradition through baptism, weddings, and *quinceañeras*. The ties of *compadrazgo* are as strong and permanent as any family connection. At Gethsemane, Mother's Day is celebrated in a context where the congregation is seen as part of this extended family. While there is no formal role for *padrinos* and *compadres* in the Presbyterian service of Baptism, similar vows are made by the congregation as a whole. It was not uncommon at Gethsemane for *compadres* to stand with the parents when their child was baptized, symbolizing their special relationship to the child and the family. The pastor would always remind the congregation when we stood to affirm our vows to support the parents and to help nurture the child in the Christian faith, that we as a community took on the responsibility of godparent, affirming our relationship as a family of God.

In this context, where family is a defining metaphor for community, Mother's Day is celebrated with special significance. The difference may be that in this context, it is the relationship of mother, and by extension, family, which is celebrated, avoiding the ambivalence of seeing motherhood as a matter of personal achievement. Another difference effected by the cultural context is the way in which Mother's Day is observed. Rather than each child having something to give to his or her own mother, the children at Gethsemane shared their gifts collectively through songs and poems for the whole congregation and flowers given to all the women present. In a very real way, this simple act symbolically affirms the promises made at their baptism that made the whole congregation adoptive parents of each child.

This model of church as an extended family may be an important one for the church as a whole in a society where the nuclear family is often fractured. In some ways it may be more consistent with the reality of "blended" families and may even offer a model for the church to envision itself as a support system for families, whatever their shape or size. The model of congregation as extended family may also be more welcoming to those who do not fit the nuclear model. It certainly changes the meaning of a "Church Family Potluck"!

The recognition within Hispanic congregations of the importance of expressing their faith through their own cultural symbols and the growing number of Protestant immigrants from Latin America are generating other changes in the Hispanic Presbyterian church. The increased demand for Latin music and for hymns written in Spanish is one example symbolic of this important shift from being a mission of the larger church, to being a self-defining, self-determining member of the Presbyterian family. Other changes, such as using tortillas for communion or putting serapes on the communion table, may seem superficial, but such symbols help remove a sense of contradiction between home and church. Where they are practiced, such symbols can send a powerful message of affirmation to a people whose cultural identity has been maligned and marginalized both inside and outside the church.

The recovery of cultural traditions that often have strong Catholic overtones is not without controversy within the Hispanic Presbyterian church. The *quinceañera* is the celebration of a girl's fifteenth birthday with a Mass or worship service where she reaffirms her Christian faith, with a large party following the service. As Dr. Gómez notes, it is also a tradition that is undergoing a process of change.[3] As this tradition becomes more common among Hispanic Presbyterians more questions are also being raised.

The first and perhaps most obvious objection raised is that the *quinceañera* is a sexist tradition. The criticism of sexism stems from the fact that it only applies to girls. The traditional function of the *quinceañera* is to profess the young woman as chaste, ready and available for marriage. The young women's male peers participate only as escorts in the procession and make no professions or promises concerning their own chastity or preparation for the monogamous commitment of Christian marriage. Hence the *quinceañera* would appear to sanction a double standard in the expectations it represents for young men and women.

The Rev. Tomás Chávez, a Presbyterian pastor, has developed a Presbyterian *quinceañera*.[4] In his accompanying discussion of the development of this liturgy, he traces the roots of this tradition to coming-of-age ceremonies among the Mayas, Aztecs, and Toltecs. At the age of fifteen, young boys became warriors and young girls were presented to the community as the potential mothers of future warriors. The separate ceremonies that marked their coming-of-age underscored the commitments and responsibilities imposed upon them as adult members of the community.

Part of the sexism that affronts us in the practice of the *quinceañera* today, I suspect, stems from the fact that we have lost its male counterpart. While I certainly would not advocate that we need to anoint our young men as warriors at the age of fifteen, the celebration of a young person's life as he or she crosses the threshold of adulthood ought to be important for both young men and women.

Across the U.S. today there are similar trends that suggest a need in young people's lives for coming-of-age rituals in which they can affirm their own goals for themselves and receive the support and affirmation of their community. A growing number of African American males are participating in ceremonies derived from African traditions. In several denominations, Christian young people are taking public vows of chastity and signing pledge cards vowing to remain virgins until they marry. These trends are largely a response to what are seen as destructive pressures on young people in our society—pressures to join a gang, use drugs, or become sexually active. These rituals recognize the need for the community to acknowledge, support, and affirm the positive choices young people make for their lives.

All of which suggests that if the *quinceañera* serves a positive social function, if it meets a need for Hispanic young people in our church, to affirm both their cultural heritage and their Christian faith, then perhaps the most constructive way to remedy the sexism in the tradition would be to include young men as active participants in the liturgy.

The liturgy of the *quinceañera* as Tomás Chávez has developed it poses another question for Presbyterians. With one important addition, the vows taken and the liturgy developed around them are very similar to the traditional confirmation service when young persons who have been baptized as infants publicly affirm their faith and claim the promises of their baptism for themselves. What is added in the *quinceañera* service is an expression of gratitude to God by the congregation for the gift of the young woman's life, and a prayer of dedication in which she asks for God's continuing guidance as she enters adulthood.

While young people are confirmed at a slightly younger age in most Presbyterian congregations, confirmation serves a similar function as the *quinceañera* in that having been confirmed, the young person is then considered an adult member of the church. In reality, however, very few thirteen-year-olds are ever asked to be deacons or serve on session. Similarly, most parents who give their daughters a *quinceañera* do not intend for them to actively start seeking a marriage partner before they are sixteen.

So what function do these rituals serve? Both mark a pivotal point in a person's life, that period of transition from child to adult. Perhaps the most significant part of the liturgy the Rev. Chávez has developed is the congregation's prayer of gratitude. If taken seriously, the *quinceañera* (or similar celebration for young males) is an opportunity for the congregation to celebrate with the young person the fruition of the promises claimed in his or her baptism as they reaffirm the young man's or woman's Christian faith. If this bridge carries traffic two ways, it suggests that confirmation might be much more significant in the life of the young person confirmed, and the congregation he or she is a part of, if it includes this sense of celebration. It suggests that the congregation ought to be fellow participants, rather than witnesses to the young person's vows. And then, perhaps we ought to follow confirmation services with a fiesta!

The changes going on in Hispanic Presbyterian congregations today challenge our denomination to open the bridges of culture to traffic in two directions, to embrace diversity, and draw into the center of the church's life, not just tolerate this life at the margins. Being inclusive means more than maintaining representation on church staffs and commissions. It means confessing the sin of confusing culture with gospel. It means becoming a mestizo church.

CHAPTER SEVEN

Raquel Gutiérrez-Achón

# An Introduction to Hispanic Hymnody

It has been said that music is praise, music is proclamation of the Word, and music is prayer. Martin Luther was the one who seems to have started us in this direction more than four hundred years ago. John and Charles Wesley, Isaac Watts, and many others knew that music was the easiest way to communicate the love of God in Christ to the worshiping community.

In order for this music to have authenticity, it has to include our cultural and linguistic roots. We cannot lose the vision of the past, or ignore other cultures, since music is the catalytic factor that unites the past and the present.

Hispanics are currently in the process of finding new ways of expressing the faith through new and perhaps more genuine musical forms. It is time to move forward and discard that which is trite, keep that which has stood the test of time and has universal appeal, and embrace, try out, and experience that which is new and truly ours.

A new Christian hymnology has risen in Latin America and in many communities in the United States, among Roman Catholics and Protestants alike. It has roots in Latin folk and popular music and most of the time reflects the social realities of the southern continent, owing much to the secular movement called the "new song." This "new song" has flourished since the '60s, but it has its roots in former decades. An avalanche of hymns and songs continues to flow, expressing in people's folklore, the hymns and songs of their happiness, concerns, and sufferings. But what is *folklore*?

The word *folklore* is an English word that means "the accumulated stories and memories of the people," and the dictionary defines *folklore* as "the traditional beliefs, customs, legends, and songs of a people, that are handed down orally from generation to generation." Folklore then is not just primitive art. The folk element does not come only from the country. There is a folk element in the cities, and there is urban as well as rural folkloric music.

Folk music does not always have to be anonymous. It comes from inside the person, famous or unknown, and it does not exclude illiterates. The best definition is probably the one by Fernando Ortiz, in the introduction to his book, *La africanía de la música folklórica cubana*—The African Element in Cuban Folk Music: "Authentic folk music could be defined as music of the basic stratum of a given society, by its own creation, or adapting a foreign one as familiar as its own."[1]

Our purpose, however, is not simply to folklorize or make autochthonous the music in our churches. If that were our only goal, we would be very far from the real purpose of music in worship, and we would be merely using the new musical form as an artificial element to entertain our people.

In his book, *La adoración: Análisis y orientación,* Dr. Miguel Angel Darino devotes a chapter, "Music and Its Value in Worship," to the relation between music and the Holy Spirit according to the Epistle to the Ephesians. The line of thought in that epistle is that the Holy Spirit in us is the one who enables us to express our praise to God, and therefore we have no other choice than to "sing and make melody in our hearts to the Lord" (Eph. 5:19 paraphrased).[2]

Dr. Darino is concerned about the common practice in some Hispanic churches of taking secular music, and even songs that are known for their immoral words, and setting Christian lyrics to them, to be sung in worship services. Dr. Darino continues:

> Hence the importance of not dedicating to God [in worship] music inspired under influences other than the Holy Spirit. Especially in our Hispanic context, where we are slowly seeking to bring into our practice of worship our autochthonous music, we may use the richness of rhythms and styles by creating anew, rather than by copying. We do not seek to "spiritualize" what is secular by attaching "Christian words" to existing music.[3]

Despite hundreds of articles, the language about autochthonous church music is still a subject of misinterpretation, for the process goes through a number of stages. At a lecture delivered in Pasadena some years ago, the distinguished scholar, I-to Loh, who is known worldwide, pointed out that most hymnic styles have gone through these five fundamental periods: (a) Reproduction; (b) Imitation; (c) Searching for identity; (d) New style trying to emerge [hybrid product]; and

(e) Mature artistic expression. At each of these stages, language referring to autochthonous hymnody has different meanings.

Therefore, among my colleagues who for years have explored our hymnody and its origins, there is a duality of thought concerning the existence of a Hispanic American hymnology as such. Some are of the opinion that we do not have a developed hymnology, but only popular songs, with autochthonous backgrounds. According to this opinion, what we have are isolated efforts with great regional flavor, reflecting the folk influence of each country. They would say that whatever has been accomplished is still in its initial stages. Others think that authentic forms of Hispanic hymnody have been established by hymns such as those by Pablo Sosa, Cesáreo Gabaraín, Rosa Martha Zárate, the late Skinner Chávez-Melo, and many more.

It used to be that in all this prolific production the Anglo-Saxon influence prevailed, generally reflecting the type of theology that our missionaries brought to us. That theology became part of our Protestant religious culture, which is bound together with that fundamentalist and conservative Christianity that came to us through the missionary movement. In those early hymnodic attempts, that theology was often reflected; but that is generally no longer the case.

Victor Rivera-García, in his article "Contextualized Worship: A Hispanic Approach to Mission," writes that "Christians mold and shape their own worship activities according to their perception of God and of themselves as unique cultural beings. It is the right of each culture to express worship in a way which is significant and meaningful to them."[4] And he goes on to say that Hispanic worship should seek for a balance between what comes from the cultural traditions of the people and what comes from theological and spiritual tradition—including the tradition received through the missionaries.

It is not always easy to find this balance. Let me relate a personal experience of when I wanted to introduce into our church some of the hymns that Dr. Roberto Escamilla would classify as truly Hispanic music, and that express our sense of celebration.[5] It shocked my own mother, who was a very faithful Christian. She was alarmed to the point that one day after we arrived home from a Sunday service, she told me, "Just to think that after I prayed for years, that whatever talent you had you would dedicate to the Lord, you are the one now to bring the Devil to our services." It took some very careful explaining on my part to somehow be able to change (to some extent) her way of thinking. One of my strongest arguments was, of course, my growing concern to preserve our cultural heritage in our worship and our music as well. Our hymnody has been separate from the mainstream of all other music, and church music should be treated so as to be relevant to our culture. Our hymns and songs must be given expression in and by our culture.

The church has gone through political and cultural changes since the times of the first Protestant missionary contacts with our culture, and we now have to put forth a new vision of Christianity through our music. There is a social awareness and even confrontation that involve the entire life of the Hispanic church, including its music. Also, we have felt the need of having music as an effective force in the development of Christian character, so the church can be instrumental in the development and identity of Hispanic people.

In their article, "How Shall We Sing the Lord's Song in a Foreign Land? (Theological and Cultural Implications of Hispanic Liturgical Music),"[6] Celeste Burgos and Ken Mentz write that "culture will be used to describe language, values, styles and patterns of relationship." They continue saying that Hispanic liturgical music has to do with the symbiosis between a religious tradition and a particular culture; and for Hispanics in the United States, liturgical issues are not only a question of a religious tradition encountering a particular culture, but also a minority group functioning in a dominant *Anglo* culture.

If we briefly investigate the history of the church, the first Christian hymns in the Bible were born in a period of crisis. They appear in places such as the Gospel of John and in the letters of Paul. Paul establishes certain guidelines for the organization of the church, and uses hymns that appear in his letters rather like dogmatic theological tracts—probably not to be sung, but played in the background in the Hebrew style.

The first hymnals were published in the Middle Ages—particularly at the time of Pope Gregory, but also earlier collections of Ambrosian chants. Later on, the Reformation period was noted for its many hymnals. The Roman Catholic Church also published hymnals, and these were very difficult for congregations to sing, like the Psalms of Deiss and Gelineau. It has been in the last thirty years or so—partially as a result of the Second Vatican Council—that the Roman Catholic Church has become seriously interested in developing singing congregations by providing materials appropriate to that task.

Since the sacred scriptures were first distributed by Protestants in Mexico and other countries of Latin America in the first half of the nineteenth century, the influence of North American missionaries was felt in all aspects of the life of the Church, and in its music as well. Therefore it is not surprising that the hymnodic tradition of the Latin American church was based almost completely on the "gospel hymn" of the nineteenth century. An analysis and comparison of the hymnals in our churches published prior to the 1980s would clearly reveal this fact, as only a few hymnals dedicate some space to the literature that has its origin in some countries other than the United States and Great Britain, and historic periods other than the nineteenth century. The majority of the exceptions are classic hymns that have prevailed through the years, which have been frequently used in most hymnals—including those published in the nineteenth century in the United States, where "gospel hymns" dominate.

A few years ago, I was conducting a workshop in Hispanic Hymnody, and after successfully using (I thought) some of our most recently composed hymns, one of the well-known persons present, for years a leader in that church, asked me, "Sister, can we finish by singing one of our own hymns?" My heart sank when she asked for "Brighten the Corner Where You Are"!

As for the hymns in those hymnals of the early years, Kenneth Gould Greenlaw Jr. correctly says that

> if they were original compositions, they were poorly harmonized, being an effort (which should be praised) of self-taught composers. Simple harmonies like tonic-dominant, with occasionally a ninth chord, and auxiliary chromatic tones and dotted quarter and eighth note rhythm were abundant. Poetic meters in the text were irregular, so asymmetrical phrases in structure were common too.[7]

In these new times of revolutionary concepts, a need has arisen to develop a real hymnology for Hispanics. We have to build *criterios,* explore the folklore *de los pueblos,* and establish a serious evaluation in a truly objective process of selecting the hymns to be included in hymnals and sung in congregations.

Already there are hymns that have transcended barriers, and this process will eventually help to lead us to Christian unity. Cesáreo Gabaraín's hymns, as well as Pablo Sosa's, are being sung in Roman Catholic as well as Protestant churches everywhere Spanish is spoken. Significant changes have taken place in our worship services. Many denominations are having their official hymnals revised, and resources come off the press constantly, with spontaneous outpouring from the hearts of the people. New poetic materials give expression to certain new emphases in religious thought of the present day. We hope that all this music will bring about significant and creative interest not only among Hispanics, but also among non-Hispanics, who will benefit from this production.

Some of the objectives that can be accomplished, as we nurture our people and others to "cultivate" this production, are:

1. To *encourage and pursue* the high values of this church music, and its importance in the theological expression of faith.
2. To *equip and empower* Hispanics with the necessary skills for the development of indigenous hymnology.
3. To *explore* ways by which this music can relate to the whole community, thus enhancing the lifestyle of Hispanics in the United States.

Men and women are creatures whose lives are seasoned by variety, with a need for something to break the daily routine. Therefore, if our worship is celebration and joy (that joy coming from the Holy Spirit as I mentioned before), our music and our hymns must be dynamic, containing elements of change and innovation.

What can we say about the different styles of this outpouring of creativity? Unexpected rhythms are part of the so-called asymmetrical character of Hispanic music. There are similarities, as well as outstanding differences in styles, from region to region.

The music from the Caribbean countries has a very strong African influence, as in the well-known "cross-rhythms pattern," which is nothing but the polyrhythmic sound of the African drums. I can remember in Cuba listening to Black people playing their music, where each drum was beating to a different rhythm. Nevertheless, there was a "central beat," so to speak, common to them all. This is common, too, in the music that comes to us from Brazil. Africans brought to the Caribbean and Brazil were of the Sudanese and Bantu cultures, and this influence can still be felt in their descendants as well as in general in the cultures of the areas where they lived.

The Andean countries—Peru, Bolivia, and Ecuador—reflect much of the indigenous element. Many of their melodies are minor. It could be that they still identify with Gregorian melodies, which were the first ones they were acquainted with, or maybe they want to express the mysticism that church music was always meant to express. Nevertheless, all the resurrection hymns are in major.

Brazil and Argentina reflect more variety in style. Both countries use folklore, popular North American music, and European four-part harmony (almost classic), while in Brazil they have emphasized the descending melodic line. Much of their church music is more sophisticated musically than that of other countries, and we can also say this of Argentina, where the tonal duality and rhythm/structure are written in 6/8 time, alternating closely with 3/4 time. Venezuela uses more complex rhythms, and they generally change from major to minor or vice versa, as is typical of the Copla Andaluza.

Central America, except Guatemala and El Salvador, has hardly given us Hispanic hymns. Their cultural influence tends to be Mexican or South American. Mexicans, as well as Texan-Mexicans, have a great affinity with North American music. They are, generally speaking, more conservative, using fewer folklore elements, simple melodies, and simple patterns repeated in melody and harmony. Melodies often repeat in thirds, as in the Misa Mariachi by Lojewski.

Some of the best music that comes to us is from Spain. It is rich in melody and harmony. Nevertheless, one can discern the Hispanic cadences, and sometimes simple melodic lines that reflect the impact of seven hundred years of Moorish presence.

In addition to these, Hispanic musicians have adopted some other rhythms, for example, the calypso from the Virgin Islands.

Most Hispanic hymns begin with the chorus or *estribillo,* which is repeated after each stanza and sometimes twice at the beginning and twice at the end. In general, texts communicate a challenge to deeper faith, the need to fight for justice, and salvation as a process.

Quoting from Bishop Federico J. Pagura: "Tenemos Esperanza (We Have Hope)"

> In hope we are forever celebrating;
> with courage in our struggle we are waiting.
> In trust and reassurance we are claiming.
> This is our song of freedom for all people.
> In hope we are forever celebrating;
> with courage in our struggles we are waiting.
> In trust and reassurance we are claiming.
> This is our song.[8]

> ("Tenemos Esperanza [We Have Hope]" is reprinted with permission from Discipleship Resources, Nashville, TN.)

The gospel makes us free, even as we face defeat; let us then proclaim that Christ is still "in charge of history" in our culture, and our music must reflect that fact.

*Soli Deo gloria.*

# Appendix

Pablo A. Jiménez

# Worship Resources

Hispanics have an old, rich, and diverse culture. As we have seen throughout the book, devotional piety is expressed in various ways in the Latino community. The aim of this Appendix is to offer a glimpse of those rich worship traditions.

This section opens with two important documents. The first is an affirmation of faith titled *Nuestro Credo: Un Credo Hispano*. It was written by Justo L. González for *Mil voces para celebrar*, the new United Methodist hymnal in Spanish. The English version is also provided. The second is *A Thanksgiving Litany*, inspired by essays of Puerto Rican schoolchildren in New York City. These documents convey celebration of our diverse Hispanic roots, solidarity with the Latino community, and a commitment with the all-inclusive Reign of God.

This section also includes three hymns and four *coritos* or *estribillos*. The first hymn, titled *"Las Posadas"* ("The Inns"), illustrates the Catholic devotional piety tradition reviewed in chapter 2 by Allan Figueroa Deck. Please note that this is an English version of some of the traditional Spanish words, set to the familiar tune of "Good King Wenceslas." Traditionally, a group goes from house to house being rejected, and is finally accepted at a house where all are fed. This song could be used in that way, or also adapted for a church supper, where Mary and Joseph seek a place from table to table, and are finally accepted at one of them. It may also be used as part of the traditional dramatizations during the season of Christmas.

The second hymn, *"Padre Nuestro"* ("The Lord's Prayer"), was written by Carlos Rosas and is part of his *Mexican-American Mass*. Since the words are familiar, it could be sung in Spanish even by those who do not know the language. Or, it could easily be adapted to be sung to the Lord's Prayer in English.

The third, titled *"Doquier haya almas reunidas"* ("Wherever Souls Are Gathered"), is a Puerto Rican hymn written by Ramón (Moncho) Díaz during the Great Revival that rocked the island in the 1930s. It celebrates the joy of gathering for worship.

The four *coritos* or *estribillos* are lively anonymous works that pass by word of mouth from one congregation to another. Usually, worshipers learn them by heart and musicians improvise their melody. For this reason, there are as many versions of these as churches that sing them. The first one is a Panamanian anthem titled *"Arriba los Corazones"* ("Lift Up Your Hearts"). This song is traditionally used by denominations where Holy Communion is central to the worship experience, such as for Catholics, Anglicans, and Lutherans. The other *coritos* are closely based on biblical texts. *"La palabra del Señor"* ("The Lord's Word") is based on Isa. 55:11 and Luke 19:40. The emphasis on the Word reveals its Reformed background. The two remaining pieces are *"Alabad a Jehová"* ("Praise the

Lord") and *"Te alabarán, oh Jehová, todos los reyes"* ("All the Kings of the Earth Shall Praise You, Oh Lord"). They are based on Pss. 117 and 138:4-6, respectively. Although both are widely used, they are characteristic of Hispanic Pentecostal worship.

# NUESTRO CREDO

## Un Credo Hispano

Creemos en Dios Padre Todopoderoso,
  creador de los cielos y de la tierra;
  creador de los pueblos y las culturas;
  creador de los idiomas y de las razas.

Creemos en Jesucristo, su Hijo, nuestro Señor,
  Dios hecho carne en un ser humano para todos los humanos;
  Dios hecho carne en un momento para todas las edades;
  Dios hecho carne en una cultura para todas las culturas.
  Dios hecho carne en amor y gracia para toda la creación.

Creemos en el Espíritu Santo,
  por quien el Dios encarnado en Jesucristo
    se hace presente en nuestro pueblo y nuestra cultura;
  por quien el Dios creador de todo cuanto existe
    nos da poder para ser nuevas criaturas;
  quien con sus infinitos dones, nos hace un solo pueblo:
    el cuerpo de Jesucristo.

Creemos en la Iglesia,
  que es universal porque es señal del Reino Venidero,
  que es más fiel mientras más se viste de colores;
  donde todos los colores pintan un mismo paisaje;
  donde todos los idiomas cantan una misma alabanza.

Creemos en el Reino Venidero, día de la Gran Fiesta,
  cuando todos los colores de la creación
    se unirán en un arco iris de armonía;
  cuando todos los pueblos de la tierra
    se unirán en un banquete de alegría;
  cuando todas las lenguas del universo
    se unirán en un coro de alabanza.

Y porque creemos, nos comprometemos
  a creer por los que no creen,
  a amar por los que no aman,
  a soñar por los que no sueñan,
  hasta que lo que esperamos se torne realidad. Amén.

Justo L. González
© 1994 Abingdon Press

# Hispanic Creed*

We believe in God, the Father Almighty
Creator of the heavens and the earth;
Creator of all peoples and all cultures;
Creator of all tongues and races.

We believe in Jesus Christ, his Son, our Lord,
God made flesh in a person for all humanity,
God made flesh in an age for all the ages,
God made flesh in one culture for all cultures,
God made flesh in love and grace for all creation.

We believe in the Holy Spirit
through whom God incarnate in Jesus Christ
makes his presence known in our peoples and our cultures;
through whom, God Creator of all that exists,
gives us power to become new creatures;
whose infinite gifts make us one people:
the Body of Christ.

We believe in the Church
    universal because it is a sign of God's Reign,
    whose faithfulness is shown in its many hues
    where all the colors paint a single landscape,
    where all tongues sing the same praise.

We believe in the Reign of God—the day of the Great Fiesta
    when all creation's colors will form a harmonious rainbow,
    when all peoples will join in joyful banquet,
    when all tongues of the universe will sing the same song.

And because we believe, we commit ourselves:
    to believe for those who do not believe,
    to love for those who do not love,
    to dream for those who do not dream,
until the day when hope becomes reality.

*by Justo González

*115*

# A THANKSGIVING LITANY

*(Inspired by essays of Puerto Rican schoolchildren in New York City, published by the Foundation for Change)*

**Leader:** We thank you, God.

**People:** We thank you, God, for who we are.

**Leader:** Some of us look like the people who lived here long ago, so close to this land that their arrival is not recorded.

**People:** We thank you, God, for who we are.

**Leader:** Some of us look like the people who lived here long ago, so close to this land that their arrival is not recorded.

**People:** We thank you, God, for who we are.

**Leader:** Some of us look like the Spanish, who came in big ships. They took the land from the Indians and the Spanish, and thought it was theirs.

**People:** We thank you, God, for who we are.

**Leader:** Some of us look like the Africans, who also came in bit ships. They did not choose to come, and they had no land and no freedom.

**People:** We thank you, God, for who we are.

**Leader:** Some of us look like the Asians, who came in big ships across the other ocean. They came looking for work and freedom, and many found discrimination and injustice.

**People:** We thank you, God, for who we are.

**Leader:** All of us are different. No two of us look exactly alike. But we are all in the image of God, who came to earth that we might be one.

**People:** We thank you, God, for who we are, and we pray that you show us what we are to be. Amen.

From *In Accord: Let Us Worship* edited by Justo L. and Catherine G. González. Copyright © 1981 by Friendship Press, Inc., New York. Used by permission.

# Las Posadas *(The Inns)*

*Joseph* { 1. In the name of God we beg: will you let us en - ter?
*and* { 2. It is not by our own choice that to - day we tra - vel.
*Mary* { 3. Will the child be born to - night out on a street cor - ner?

We are tired and we are cold. May we please have shel - ter?
But the Em - per - or has said that all must be count - ed.
Can't you find a place for him? Do you have no pi - ty?

*The* You look dir - ty and you smell. Will you please keep mov - ing?
*inn-* For your rea - sons we care not. Ev - 'ry - room is tak - en.
*keepers* Oh my good-ness, do come in. You can use the man - ger.

For your kind there is no place, for our inn is de - cent.
Can't you see the place is full? You are bad for bus - i - ness.
For the rooms that we do have are for a rich trav' - ler.

WORDS: Trans. and adapt. by J. L. Gonzalez
MUSIC: From *Piae Cantiones*, 1582; harm. by Ernest MacMillan, 1893

TEMPUS ADEST FLORIDUM
76.76 D

# Padre Nuestro

Pa-dre nues - tro que es-tás en el cie - lo,

san - ti - fi - ca-do, san - ti - fi - ca-do se - a tu nom-bre.

Ven - ga - nos Tu rei-no, Se - ñor; há - ga -

se tu san-ta vo-lun - tad en el cie-lo y en la tie - rra. Ha -

re-mos tu San-ta vo-lun - tad. Pa-dre nues -

tro que es-tás en el cie - lo, san - ti - fi - ca-do,

san - ti - fi - ca-do se - a tu nom-bre.

Da - nos hoy, Dá-nos-lo, Se - ñor, nues - tro pan, el

WORDS: Carlos Rosas
MUSIC: Carlos Rosas
© 1976 by the Mexican American Cultural Center

pan de ca - da dí - a y per - do - na nues-tras deu-das a - sí co-mo no -

so-tros per-do - na-mos. Pa-dre nues - tro

que es-tás en el cie - lo, san - ti - fi - ca-do,

san - ti - fi - ca-do se - a tu nom-bre.

No nos de-jes ca - er en ten-ta - ción; an - tes bien,

lí - bra-nos del mal. No nos de-jes ca - er en ten-ta - ción, lí - bra -

nos del mal. Pa-dre nues - tro

que es-tás en el cie - lo, san - ti - fi - ca-do, san - ti - fi -

ca-do se - a tu nom-bre.

# Doquier haya almas reunidas

1. Do - quier ha - ya al - mas reu - ni - das, do -
2. Do - quie - ra Je - sús se pre - sen - ta, a -

quier ha - ya go - zo y a-mor, se sien - te más gra - ta la
li - via el pe-sar y el do - lor; en me - dio de lu - chas y

vi - da lo - an - do a Je-sús el Se - ñor.
ma - les, el o - dio se tor - na en a - mor.

Se i - nun - da de jú - bi-lo el al - ma, se
Por e - so can - ta - mos a - le - gres, por

sien - te la gran ben-di - ción; paz san - ta que da dul-ce
e - so de - ci - mos a - sí; la fe del Se-ñor da a -

LETRA: Ramón Díaz, ca. 1934
MUSICA: Ramón Díaz, ca. 1934; arreg. de Carmen Peña
Arreg. © 1996 Abingdon Press

PRESENCIA RENOVADORA
98.98 D y coro

cal - ma        al  po - bre  y  dé - bil co - ra - zón.
lien - to;      sa - be - mos que El es - tá a - quí.

Ya sen - ti - mos a - quí    la pre - sen - cia del Se - ñor,  la sen -

ti - mos; sí,  nos i - nun - da su luz.    Ya    las al - mas re -

vi - ven      y    se a - le - gra el co - ra - zón;

a - quí es - tá Cris - to el Ma - es - tro,  a - quí hay ben - di - ción.

# Arriba los Corazones

¡A - rri-ba los co - ra - zo - nes! Va-ya-mos to - dos al pan de vi -
da, que es fuen-te de glo - ria e-ter - na, de for - ta - le -
za y de a - le - grí - a.

*Estribillo*

A ti a - cu - di - mos se - dien - tos.
Que - re - mos dar - te la vi - da.

¡Ven Se - ñor! Te - ne-mos fe en tu mis - te - rio. ¡Ven Se - ñor!
¡Ven Se - ñor! Con sus do - lo - res y di - chas. ¡Ven Se - ñor!

LETRA: Autor desconocido
MUSICA: Tradicional panameña

# La palabra del Señor

① La pa - la-bra del Se-ñor no vuel-ve a El va - cí - a. ¡A - mén, ②

③ a - mén! Si no - so-tros ca - llá-ra-mos las pie-dras cla-ma-rí - an. ¡A - mén, ④

a - mén! ¡A - mén, a - mén, a - mén,

a - mén! ¡A - mén, a - mén, a - mén, a - mén!

LETRA: Isaías 55:11; Lucas 19:40
MUSICA: Autor desconocido

122

# Alabad a Jehová

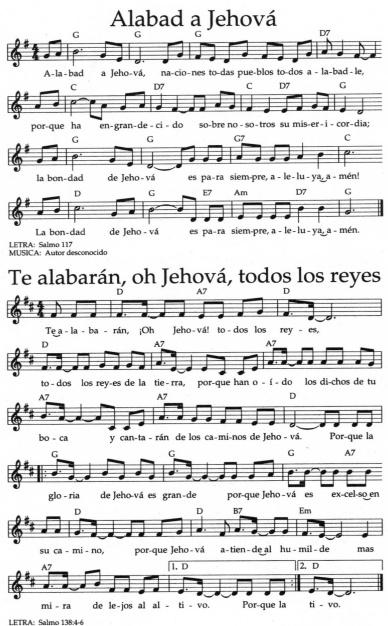

A-la-bad a Jeho-vá, na-cio-nes to-das pue-blos to-dos a - la-bad - le,
por-que ha en-gran-de - ci - do so-bre no - so-tros su mis-er-i - cor-dia;
la bon-dad de Jeho-vá es pa-ra siem-pre, a - le-lu - ya, a - mén!
La bon-dad de Jeho - vá es pa-ra siem-pre, a - le-lu - ya, a - mén.

LETRA: Salmo 117
MUSICA: Autor desconocido

# Te alabarán, oh Jehová, todos los reyes

Te a - la - ba - rán, ¡Oh Jeho-vá! to - dos los rey - es,
to - dos los rey-es de la tie - rra, por-que han o - í - do los di-chos de tu
bo - ca y can-ta - rán de los ca-mi-nos de Jeho - vá. Por-que la
glo - ria de Jeho-vá es gran-de por-que Jeho-vá es ex-cel-so en
su ca - mi - no, por-que Jeho - vá a-tien-de al hu - mil - de mas
mi - ra de le-jos al al - ti - vo. Por-que la ti - vo.

1. D        2. D

LETRA: Salmo 138:4-6
MUSICA: Autor desconocido

*123*

# NOTES

## 1. Hispanic Worship: An Introduction

1. On this point, see my article, "A New People Is Born," in Daniel R. Rodriguez-Diaz and David Cortés-Fuentes, *Hidden Stories: Unveiling the History of the Latino Church* (Decatur, Ga.: Asociación para la Educación Teológica Hispana, 1994), pp. 101-105.

2. In this respect, the Hispanic Association of Bilingual Bicultural Ministries (HABBM) plays an important role, at least among Protestants. At a conference held on August 26, 1995, Luis Madrigal, Executive Director of HABBM, pointed to this generational and cultural gap: "These young people are frustrated because most Hispanic churches are Spanish-only and dominated by their parents' culture. . . . Pastors, on the other hand, want to keep young people in the church, but often don't understand why these young people—even their own children—are so different from them."

3. For a description of these and other elements in popular religiosity, see chapter 2.

4. *Testimonios* and *coritos* are discussed in chapter 3. For further explanation of *coritos*, see also chapters 4 and 7, as well as the glossary.

5. Additional descriptions of *compadres* and *compadrazgo* can be found in chapter 6, and in the glossary.

6. This idea is found in one of the seminal books for Latino theology in the United States: Virgilio Elizondo, *Galilean Journey: The Mexican-American Promise* (Maryknoll, N.Y.: Orbis, 1983).

7. See, for instance, Margarita Sánchez de León, "African-American Woman," in *Hidden Stories*, pp. 113-16. Some of the theoretical foundation for this sort of reflection may be seen in Héctor E. López-Sierra, "Un acercamiento postmoderno al protestantismo popular latinoamericano y caribeño," *Apuntes*, Year 14, no. 1 (spring 1994), pp. 19-26.

8. See John H. Elliott, *A Home for the Homeless: A Social-Scientific Criticism of I Peter, Its Situation and Strategy* (Minneapolis: Fortress, 1990).

9. *To Diognetus*, 5.5.

## 2. Hispanic Catholic Prayer and Worship

1. Rosa María Icaza is one of the more accomplished writers in this field. See her recent article, "Prayer, Worship and Liturgy in a U.S. 'Hispanic Key,' " in *Frontiers of Hispanic Theology in the United States*, ed. A. Figueroa Deck, S. J. (Maryknoll, N.Y.: Orbis, 1992), pp. 134-53. See also Germán Martínez, O.S.B.,

"Hispanic Culture and Worship: The Process of Inculturation," in *U.S. Catholic Historian,* vol. 2 (no. 2, spring 1993), pp. 79-91.

2. Orlando O. Espín has made several contributions to our contemporary understanding of Hispanic popular Catholicism. See for example, "Tradition and Popular Religion: An Understanding of the *Sensus Fidelium,*" in *Frontiers of Hispanic Theology,* pp. 62-87.

3. There are many fascinating studies of the process by which aspects of the Christian message were grafted onto the cultures of native Americans and incarnated in popular rituals and forms of prayer. Robert Ricard's *The Spiritual Conquest of Mexico* (Berkeley: University of California Press, 1981) is a classic treatment originally done in the 1920s. More recently, anthropologist John M. Ingham studied the long, complex process by which the peoples of Central Mexico incorporated Christian orthodoxy into their worldview in *Mary, Michael and Lucifer* (Austin: University of Texas Press, 1989).

4. One of the useful resources for the study of the popular religious practices of Hispanic Catholics, especially those of Mexican origin, is *Faith Expressions of Hispanics in the Southwest,* ed. Luis Maldonado (San Antonio: Mexican-American Cultural Center Book Store, 1990).

5. See Segundo Galilea, *Religiosidad Popular y Pastoral Latinoamericana* (New York: Northeast Hispanic Catholic Pastoral Center, Inc., 1981).

6. The tendency of some evangelical Christian congregations to admit traditional forms of Hispanic Catholic devotion in their prayer and worship is noted by three current researchers: E. King, *Final Report on the Attitudes Toward Proselytism of Ethnic Minorities* (Washington, D.C.: Committee for Applied Research on the Apostolate/Georgetown University, 1988); G. Padilla, "Proselytism, Conservatism and the Hispanics," in *Pastoral Life,* November 1989, pp. 13-21; and J. Diaz-Vilar in "The Success of the Sects Among Hispanics in the United States," *America,* no. 160, 1989, pp. 174-81.

7. See A. Figueroa Deck, "Latino Theology: The Year of the Boom," in *The Journal of Hispanic/Latino Theology,* vol. 1, no. 2 (February 1994), pp. 51-63.

8. See Harvey Cox, "Carnival Faith," in *Religion in the Secular City* (New York: Simon and Schuster, 1984), pp. 61-79.

9. A professor at the Evangelical Faculty of Orlando E. Costas in Lima, Peru, discusses the criticisms against Hispanic popular Catholicism made by various Protestant experts and suggests that today some evangelicals are not as sure as they used to be about some of the criticisms made of this popular religion. See also Tito Paredes, "Popular Religiosity: A Protestant Perspective," *Missiology,* vol. 20, no. 2 (April 1992), pp. 205-20.

10. Cox, "Carnival Faith," pp. 240-61.

11. See V. Fagone, "La religione Popolare in Gramsci," *La Civiltà Catolica,* no. 3 (1978), pp. 530-46.

12. Paredes, "Popular Religiosity," p. 214.

13. A new and extensive study of the medieval characteristics of Mexican culture and the persistence of certain religious styles and sensibilities rooted in Catholic Spain is Luis Weckmann *The Medieval Heritage of Mexico* (New York: Fordham University Press, 1992).

14. See A. Figueroa Deck, "The Appeal of Evangelical/Pentecostal Christianity to Hispanic Catholics," in *Hispanic Catholics: Issues and Concerns* (Notre Dame, Ind.: University of Notre Dame Press, 1994).

15. In his book, Eldin Villafañe, a leading Hispanic Pentecostal theologian, has produced an original outline of a "Pentecostal social ethic." To do so, he used as primary resource United States Hispanic and Latin American theology, much of it Roman Catholic. See *The Liberating Spirit* (Grand Rapids, Mich.: Eerdmans, 1993).

### 3. Hispanic Pentecostal Worship

1. See David Martin, *Tongues of Fire: The Explosion of Protestantism in Latin America* (London: Basil Blackwell Press, 1991).

2. Larry Tye, "Tongues of Fire," *The Boston Globe,* 15 November 1994, pp. 16-17.

3. Ibid.

4. Donald W. Dayton, *Theological Roots of Pentecostalism* (Peabody, Mass.: Hendrickson Publications, 1987).

5. Among Pentecostals of the Church of God (Cleveland, Tennessee), which is the third largest Pentecostal body, ritual foot washing is recognized as one of the three sacraments commanded by Christ along with water baptism and the Eucharist.

6. Orlando E. Costas, *Christ Outside the Gate: Mission Beyond Christendom* (New York: Orbis, 1982).

7. Virgilio Elizondo, *The Galilean Journey: The Mexican-American Promise* (New York: Orbis, 1985).

8. José Vasconcelos, *La raza cósmica: La misión de la raza iberoamericana* (Barcelona: Espasa-Calpe, 1925).

9. This list is not intended to be all-inclusive of the various parts of the worship service. It is meant to highlight some of the more important aspects. For instance, no mention is made of offerings. Yet like most services, this too is part of a Hispanic Pentecostal worship service. Offerings are especially important in light of the fact that Hispanic Pentecostal congregations are generally self-supporting, self-propagating, and self-governing.

10. This book is published in several editions by Editorial Vida, in Miami.

### 4. Worship in the Hispanic United Methodist Church

1. Comité Organizador de la Celebración del CCL Aniversario del nacimiento del Rev. Juan Wesley, *La Iglesia Metodista de México y su Herencia Wesleyena* (Mexico City: 1953), p. 148.

2. Roberto L. Gómez, "Mestizo Spirituality: Motifs of Sacrifice, Transformation, Thanksgiving, and Family in Four Mexican-American Rituals," *Apuntes,* Year 11, vol. 4 (winter 1991), p. 89.

3. Ibid., p. 87.

4. During my childhood and teen years our church used *Himnos de alabanza, pureza y poder, Himnos de gloria, Cantos de triunfo, Himnos de la vida cristiana, El nuevo himnario evangélico, Himnos selectos,* as well as a few more.
5. Alfredo Náñez, *Himnario Metodista* (San Antonio: Rio Grande Conference Board of Education, 1956), p. v.
6. These resources included responsive readings, creeds, a lectionary, and a table of special religious days (Ash Wednesday, Easter, Pentecost, first Sunday in Advent, and the number of Sundays in each season of the Christian year from 1906 through the year 2000).
7. The Division of Evangelism, Worship, and Stewardship of the General Board of Discipleship in Nashville, Tennessee, published a book with twenty-three *estribillos* arranged by Esther Frances. Many of these *estribillos* were orally transmitted, so there was no known written music for many of them. Most of them are by unknown composers.
8. Roberto Escamilla, ed., *Celebramos II* (Nashville: The United Methodist Publishing House, 1983), p. iv.

### 5. What Is Different About Hispanic Baptist Worship?

1. Pablo A. Deiros and Carlos Mraida, *Latinoamérica en Llamas* (Miami: Editorial Caribe, 1994), pp. 84-96.
2. Antonio Bentué, *La Cultura O Dios* (Salamanca, Spain: Ediciones Sígueme, 1982), pp. 32-33.
3. G. Thomas Halbrooks, in *The Complete Library of Christian Worship,* vol. 2, *Twenty Centuries of Christian Worship,* Robert E. Webber, editor (Nashville: Star Song Publishing Group, 1994), p. 293.
4. A significant example of such efforts is academic courses such as "Towards an Authentic Hispanic Worship" (Hacia un culto hispano auténtico), which have been offered for more than five years at Northern Baptist Theological Seminary in Lombard, Illinois.
5. H. H. Muirhead, *Historia del Cristianismo,* vol. 3 (El Paso: Casa Bautista de Publicaciones, 1957), p. 119.
6. The Protestant Reformation stands out in the history of Western Christianity as an exciting, revolutionary, and especially creative time. But in regards to worship, the Reformers certainly did not show the same creativity as they did in doctrine and church government.
7. Halbrooks in Webber, *The Complete Library of Christian Worship,* p. 292.
8. Franklin M. Segler, *Christian Worship: Its Theology and Practice* (Nashville: Broadman Press, 1967), p. 46.
9. Henry C. Vedder, *A Short History of the Baptists* (Philadelphia: American Baptist Publication Society, 1907), p. 203.
10. Ernest A. Payne, *The Fellowship of Believers* (London: The Carey Kingsgate Press Ltd., 1954), pp. 92-93.
11. Both John Smyth and Thomas Helwys were opposed to the use of congregational singing. They believed that singing as a gift was to be exercised only

individually. Congregational singing was not established among the Baptists until the days of Benjamin Keach, an outstanding Baptist pastor in London. For more extensive details consult Payne, *The Fellowship of Believers*, p. 93.

12. Ibid., p. 95.

13. Justo Anderson, *Historia de los Bautistas*, vol. 2 (El Paso: Casa Bautista de Publicaciones, 1994), pp. 54-55.

14. Halbrooks, in Webber, *The Complete Library of Christian Worship*, pp. 232-35.

15. In Joe R. Stacker and Wesley Forbis, eds., *Authentic Worship: Exalting God and Reaching People* (Nashville: Convention Press, 1990), p. 126.

16. Ibid., pp. 14-15.

17. Vedder, *A Short History of the Baptists*, pp. 288-89.

18. Anderson, *Historia de los Bautistas*, p. 112.

19. Ibid.

20. In my book, *La adoración: Análisis y orientación* (Cupertino, Calif.: Distribuidora Internacional de Materiales Evangélicos, 1992), pp. 18-20, I briefly point out the missionary currents and influences that took the gospel and the style or models of worship to our people.

21. The word *subculture* is used by Ricardo Chartier when he refers to the Protestant manifestations in Latin America, developed in the face of the institutionalized traditional religion. See: *Culto: Crítica y Búsqueda*, ed. Carlos E. Valle (Buenos Aires: Centro de Estudios Cristianos, 1972).

22. An important analysis of what happened in the '60s in the North American context can be found in "Baptists in the Twentieth Century," a paper presented at the Baptist Historical Society, by K. W. Clements, July 1982, pp. 21-30.

23. Darino, *La adoración: Análisis y orientación*, p. 73.

24. I am not referring specifically to Baptists, but more to what happens in general in Anglo churches. Charles Colson in his book *The Body: Being Light in the Darkness* (Dallas: Word Publishing, 1992), p. 341, mentions this fact. A Baptist independent church, Willow Creek Community Church, conducted a very interesting survey in the suburbs of Chicago. One of the questions was: "Why don't you go to church?" Two common answers were: "Because the services are boring and repetitive," and "Because what is preached has no relation to daily life."

25. An interesting summary of the Baptist distinctives can be found in "Afirmación de nuestras raíces bautistas," by Dr. Eduardo Font, in *Avance Bautista Hispano*, American Baptist Churches, USA, Valley Forge, Pa., November 1979.

26. Warren W. Wiersbe, *Real Worship* (Nashville: Oliver-Nelson, 1986), p. 106.

27. For more development of this theme, see Stacker and Forbis, *Authentic Worship*, p. 26.

### 6. Becoming a Mestizo Church

1. Justo L. González, *Mañana: Christian Theology from a Hispanic Perspective* (Nashville: Abingdon Press, 1990), p. 96. The image of the bridge to describe the relationship between culture and worship is borrowed from González, who

uses it to describe the reciprocal effect on Christian theology of the early church's outreach to the Greco-Roman world. The imagery is a fruitful one for exploring the connections, and understanding the oppressive nature of evangelism when the gate is closed on one end, imposing the culture of the missionary as though it were the good news itself and rendering those at the receiving end invisible.

2. Dr. Roberto Gómez, "Mestizo Spirituality: Motifs of Sacrifice, Transformation, Thanksgiving, and Family in Four Mexican-American Rituals," *Apuntes*, Year 11, vol. 4 (winter 1991), p. 86.

3. Ibid., pp. 85-87.

4. Tomás Chávez Jr., *Quinceañera: A Liturgy in the Reformed Tradition* (booklet, n. p.: 1982). The Rev. Chávez, now retired, was pastor of Iglesia Presbiteriana Nazareth in San Angelo, Texas, and Staff Associate for the Presbytery of Tres Rios when he wrote the booklet and had it printed in January 1982. I am indebted to the Rev. Daniel M. Garza, Director of Racial Ethnic Ministries at Austin Presbyterian Theological Seminary, for obtaining a copy of this material for me.

### 7. An Introduction to Hispanic Hymnody

1. Fernando Ortiz, *La africanía de la música folklórica cubana* (Havana, Cuba: Ministerio de Educación, 1950), p. 16.

2. Miguel Angel Darino, *La adoración: Análisis y orientación* (Cupertino, Calif.: Distribuidora Internacional de Materiales Evangélicos, 1992).

3. Ibid., p. 73.

4. Víctor Rivera-García, "Contextualized Worship: A Hispanic Approach to Mission," *¿Qué Pasa?*, a publication of the Hispanic Commission, Synod of Southern California and Hawaii of the Presbyterian Church in the U.S.A., 1988.

5. Roberto Escamilla, "Fiesta Worship," *The Interpreter* 20 (June 1976), p. 2.

6. In *Faith and Forms*, vol. 22, spring 1989, pp. 16-18.

7. Kenneth Gould Greenlaw Jr., "Traditions of Protestant Hymnody and the Use of Music in the Methodist and Baptist Churches of Mexico" (D.M.A. diss., University of Southern California, 1968), p. 5.

8. In *Celebremos, segunda parte: Colección de himnos, salmos y cánticos para suplementar el Himnario Metodista* (Nashville: Discipleship Resources, 1983), no. 31.

# GLOSSARY

**Criterio.** A word meaning criterion as well as good sense. To have good *criterio* means both to have high standards and to know how to apply them wisely.

**Bongo drums.** Drums of African origin, used all over the Caribbean for typical rhythms.

**Comadre; compadre.** Literally, co-mother and co-father. Those who stand as godparents for a child become joined to the child's family, becoming *compadres* and *comadres* with the child's parents.

**Compadrazgo.** The relationship between "co-parents" (see above, *comadre; compadre*). This relationship is considered as significant as blood ties, and establishes certain commitments and obligations between both parties.

**Congrís.** Cuban dish consisting of beans and rice cooked together.

**Coritos.** Also called *estribillos*. These are fairly simple tunes, often with repetitive words, that the people sing by heart. Most of them are anonymous, and pass by word of mouth from one congregation to another. For that reason, the tune or the words of a particular corito may vary significantly from one place to another. They are often sung to the accompaniment of clapping hands, tambourines, and other instruments.

**El pésame.** Literally, "the condolences." In the context of Holy Week observances, it refers to a sermon in which the preacher dramatizes a dialogue with Mary about the crucifixion and the events leading to it (much as a visitor at a wake will speak to the bereaved about the deceased).

**Encuentro.** Literally, "meeting." In the context of Holy Week celebrations, a dramatization in which Mary meets her risen son for the first time. This often takes place on the street, as two processions—

one carrying an image of Jesus, and the other one of Mary—wind along different routes, then finally meet.

**Estribillos.** See *coritos*.

**Madrina.** Godmother. Also used in the sense of sponsor.

**Matachínes.** Persons dressed in colorful disguises, and sometimes armed with wooden swords, whose dances—often purposefully ridiculous—have been a traditional feature of carnivals and various festivities since the Middle Ages.

**Maracas.** A musical instrument made out of a gourd with a handle and filled with seeds. Held one in each hand, they are used for beating the rhythm of a tune.

**Mestizaje.** The condition of being mestizo.

**Mestizo.** Literally, "mix-breed." Originally a pejorative term, it has gained more positive valuation thanks to the work of several Mexican and Mexican-American writers—such as Virgilio Elizondo, in the field of theology. In the U.S. setting, it describes the "in-between-ness" and the sense of belonging, yet not belonging, of the person who is considered an American, but is not considered quite as American as others.

**Mofongo.** Puerto Rican dish whose main ingredient is green plantains.

**Mole.** A Mexican dish with many regional variations. The most common is the *mole poblano* (mole Puebla style), consisting of chicken in a spicy chocolate sauce.

**Mulato; mulatez.** Terms parallel to *mestizo* and *mestizaje,* but referring to the mixture of Black and White that is typical of the Caribbean and other regions of Latin America.

**Padrino.** Godfather. Also used in the sense of "sponsor."

**Papusas.** A filled tortilla dish originating in El Salvador. Fillings vary, the most common being meat or cheese.

**Pastorelas.** Popular dramatizations of the birth and infancy of Jesus, often combining elements brought by early Spanish missionaries with elements drawn from native traditions.

**Piñata.** A container filled with candy and decorated with brilliant colors. As it hangs from a tree or a beam, blindfolded children take turns at trying to break it with a stick.

**Posadas.** A Christmas practice, particularly popular in northern Mexico and the southwestern United States. Persons playing the roles of Mary and Joseph go from house to house seeking shelter, followed by an ever-increasing crowd. "Mary" and "Joseph" are repeatedly denied shelter, until they arrive at a place where a celebration has been prepared.

**Quinceañera.** A party, often quite elaborate, celebrating a girl's fifteenth birthday.

**Testimonios.** Literally, "witnesses." A common practice in Hispanic churches, both Pentecostal and others. At a particular time during the service—or in a service specially designated for the purpose—individuals stand up and tell what God has done for them. These examples are usually quite concrete, referring to a particular prayer that has been answered, or to some other significant experience.

**Via crucis.** Known in English as the "stations of the cross." In some Latino communities, these are observed outdoors with a procession that represents Jesus' climb to Calvary. Sometimes these processions conclude atop a hill with a crucifixion scene.